crewel

EMBROIDERY

crewel
EMBROIDERY

Sue Hawkins

David & Charles

For Hannah and Jo

A DAVID & CHARLES BOOK

First published in the UK in 2001

Text, designs and patterns Copyright © Sue Hawkins 2001
Photography, layout and artworks Copyright © David & Charles 2001

Sue Hawkins has asserted her right to be identified as author of this work in accordance with
the Copyright, Designs and Patents Act, 1988.

A catalogue record for this book is available from the British Library.

ISBN 0 7153 1074 7

Photography by Tim & Zoe Hill and Jon & Barbara Stewart
Stitch diagrams by Ethan Danielson
Book design by Diana Knapp

Printed in China by Leefung-Asco
for David & Charles
Brunel House   Newton Abbot   Devon

contents

introduction

CREWEL IS DEFINED in the dictionary as 'a loosely twisted two-ply worsted yarn used in fancy work and embroidery'. The word is thought to be derived from the Anglo-Saxon word *cleow* meaning 'ball of thread' which changed first to *clew* and eventually to *cruell* or *krewel*.

This beautiful style of embroidery is difficult to define because it has no particular stitch associated with it – the stitches are many and varied and overlap with those used for other embroidery techniques. What distinguishes it is the use of crewel wool, a fine, two-ply yarn which is usually worked on natural linen. Despite the variety of stitches used crewelwork is not only one of the most enjoyable kinds of needlework for the beginner but also, I believe, one of the easiest. If you are used to counted embroidery please don't be put off by the absence of the right (or even the wrong) hole to put your needle in; this freedom is what makes this particular needle art so fulfilling.

In several of the projects in this book I have used stranded cottons and silks. Strictly speaking these pieces are not crewel embroidery but surface embroidery. However, the stitches and techniques are identical and I am quite sure that in years gone by, had the wealth of threads been available that we have today, they would have been fully utilised. So feel free to use whichever threads you like, using the photographs to help you make a good colour match or selecting your own colourway.

If you decide to use your own colours for the projects in this book then take time over your selection and don't go overboard with the number you choose. The earliest surviving piece of crewelwork, the Bayeux Tapestry (actually not a tapestry at all but a huge piece of crewelwork) uses only eight colours in total but great care was taken with their selection. This shows that it is not how many colours you use that counts but how well they work together.

Crewel embroidery is a beautiful, free way of stitching and you should endeavour to express yourself as you stitch but the most important thing is that you enjoy yourself and relax. If you do this it will show in the flowing lines of your work.

chapter one

The Garden of Eden

No book of crewel embroidery could possibly be complete without flowers. In fact it probably couldn't even begin! Associated as they are with the Garden of Eden, flowers have featured in crewel work probably since the earliest times. It was hard to choose so few from so many, so I have decided to limit myself to fairly traditional English flowers, although even the rose was an import at one stage. All of my flowers have meanings: the pansy for 'thoughts', the peony for 'bashfulness' and the rose for 'love' while the carnation carries with it the mournful phrase 'alas for my poor heart'. If you think that this is too sad a flower to embroider, then think instead of the Latin name, 'dianthus', which was derived originally from the Greek: 'di' of Zeus and 'anthos' meaning flower — flower of the gods.

Peony Jacket

*T*he peony is a large, exotic-looking flower which perhaps surprisingly carries with it the meaning of bashfulness. I've created a trail to work on the collar of a jacket. Never having been one for symmetry, I added just a single leaf to the other side of the collar, but you could work the small flower here instead, if you prefer. The design would also work well on a dress or shirt or you could simply frame it, make a short bell pull or reduce its size to make a door plate. Already you will begin to see that this design is as adaptable as you care to make it.

you will need

Fabric Refer to your jacket pattern or use a 20 x 14in (50 x 35cm) rectangle of silk

DMC stranded cotton
Very light coral 3774 – 1 skein
Light coral 758 – 1 skein
Mid coral 3778 – 1 skein
Dark coral 3830 – 1 skein
Light green 3047 – 1 skein

Mid green 3013 – 1 skein
Dark green 3012 – 1 skein
Light gold 677 – 1 skein
Mid gold 676 – 1 skein
Dark gold 680 – 1 skein
Brown 632 – 1 skein

Equipment
Size 7 crewel needle
Embroidery frame

Stitches Split back stitch, long and short stitch, fly stitch, stem stitch and French knots.

Threads Use two strands of stranded cotton throughout.

Before you begin Prepare your fabric then trace the outline on to it (see page 95).

If you are using the design on a collar I suggest you cut the pattern pieces in calico or sheeting and draw the design on this so you can check that it works well and that the pattern fits before you start. Mount it in your frame. Read the general working advice on page 88.

instructions

1 Start with the main flower. Outline the outer lower petals in dark gold split back stitch. Then begin filling in the petals with a row of long and short stitch in dark gold, taking your stitches over the split back stitch. The split back stitch gives a raised effect and makes it easier to produce a straight edge with the long and short stitch. Complete these petals in mid gold long and short stitch. Outline the central lower petal in mid gold split back stitch and then fill with long and short stitch shaded from mid gold to light gold. Work the vein in mid coral stem stitch.

2 Outline the four narrow petals above this in dark coral split back stitch and fill them with matching fly stitch.

3   Work a row of very light coral split back stitch along the top edges of the large petals. Then work a row of very light coral long and short stitch along this edge and fill in the rest of the petals with long and short stitch, shading through light to mid coral at the base.

4   For the stamens use dark gold to work short straight stitches and then add a tightly packed cluster of French knots to the end of each one.

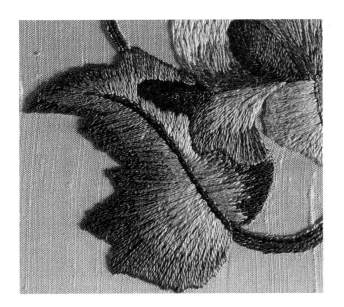

5   Now turn to the leaves next to the flower. Outline them in dark green split back stitch and then work a row of long and short stitch around the edge. Shade through mid green to light green at the centre vein. Take care where the peony overlaps each leaf, making sure that your stitches are tight against the petals with no gaps. Work the remaining leaves in the same way.

6   Move up to the flower bud. Outline the lower petals with dark gold split back stitch and then work a row of long and short stitch over it. Complete the petals with mid gold long and short stitch. Add a few matching French knots to the base of these petals for textural interest.

7   Outline the upper petals in mid coral split back stitch. Work a row of long and short stitch over it in the same colour

and then fill the rest of each petal with light coral. Work the veins in dark coral stem stitch.

8   Fill the large gaps between the petals with dark coral long and short stitch to represent the petals underneath.

9   The stems and leaf veins are worked in rows of stem stitch. For the main stem work two rows of dark green, one row of brown and one row of mid green. For the leaf veins work a row of brown and a row of dark green. Make sure you tuck the stitches tightly up against the leaf edges where the stem passes around them.

10 Finally, add a cluster of brown French knots to the top of the stem to represent a fresh bud developing.

F I N I S H I N G   O F F

When you have finished the embroidery wash and press it carefully to remove any wrinkles (see page 91). Frame the embroidery as a picture or make up your jacket as required.

A Taste of Eden

Pansies, carnations and roses are traditional English flowers which appear in paintings, tapestries and embroideries dating from many centuries ago and their images always carry with them a great deal of nostalgia. I dream of an English cottage garden myself but for now have to content myself with stitching these old favourites rather than planting the real thing. However, at least this way my 'garden' flowers all year round.

Pansy Picture

you will need

Fabric 10in (25cm) square of pure linen twill

Appleton crewel wool (yarn)
Light coral 205 – 1 skein
Dark coral 207 – 1 skein
Light green 332 – 1 skein
Mid green 334 – 1 skein

Dark green 336 – 1 skein
Light gold 695 – 1 skein
Dark gold 696 – 1 skein
Light mauve 933 – 1 skein
Dark mauve 934 – 1 skein

Equipment
Size 7 crewel needle

Size 24 tapestry needle
Embroidery hoop or frame

Stitches Long and short stitch, stem stitch, split back stitch, fly stitch, open fly stitch, straight spider's web stitch and French knots.

Threads Use one strand of crewel wool throughout.

Before you begin Prepare your fabric, then trace the outline on to it (see below). Mount it in your hoop or frame. Read the general working advice on page 88.

instructions

1 Begin with the two small leaves, outlining them in dark green split back stitch. Start to fill them with dark green long and short stitch, working over the split back stitch. The split back stitch gives a raised effect and makes it easier to produce a straight edge with the long and short stitch. Complete the leaves in long and short stitch, shading them from dark green through mid green to light green at the centre.

2 Now work the large leaf, using mid and light green long and short stitch around

the edges. Work open fly stitch in mid green up the centre gap and then outline this in light mauve stem stitch.

3 Moving on to the flower, work a split back stitch edge around the two uppermost petals in light coral and then shade them in long and short stitch, working over the split back stitch as before. Start with light coral at the edge and grade through dark coral to light mauve at the centre.

4 The three lower petals have dark mauve straight spider's web stitch edges. Lay plenty of horizontal threads. You will find it easier to change to a tapestry needle to weave the whipping thread around the bars. You can work up and down and do not worry that the first rows look uneven. You will need to weave more rows at the middle section than at each end; as the bars become full leave them out. Pack the bars tightly so they stand away from the fabric.

5 Outline the inner sections of these lower petals in dark gold using split back stitch. Fill in with long and short stitch, starting with dark gold and shading through light gold to dark mauve. Work a line of dark coral stem stitch between the dark mauve spider's web stitch and the dark gold so that the spider's web stitch looks like petal tips that have turned over.

6 Fill the centre of the flower with a tightly packed cluster of dark gold French knots.

7 Work the sepals between the petals in mid green fly stitch, outlining them first in split back stitch and working over these stitches.

8 The stem is made up of parallel lines of stem stitch in dark gold, dark and light mauve. Begin at the dark gold inner line and when you reach the tendril carry on along its length and then rejoin the main stem again at the base of the tendril. (If you work this way the tendril will look as though it grew rather than as if it was stuck on later.) Work two rows of dark mauve and one row of light mauve, adding a light mauve tendril as before. Allow the light mauve row to carry on into the two smaller

leaves to make veins. Tuck the stitches up closely against the leaf edges where the stem passes behind the large leaf.

9 Add a few French knots in dark mauve to the base of the large leaf to cover any slight gaps. This is a useful way of making two lots of stitching join together so that in this case the leaf looks as though it grew from the stem and was not just stuck on.

10 Add a small cluster of dark mauve French knots to the end of the stem to look like a cut edge.

FINISHING OFF

When you have finished the embroidery wash and press it carefully to remove any wrinkles (see page 91). Mount and frame it as required (see page 108).

Carnation Picture

you will need

Fabric 10in (25cm) square of
pure linen twill

Appleton crewel wool (yarn)
Light coral 204 – 1 skein
Mid coral 205 – 1 skein
Dark coral 207 – 1 skein
Red 725 – 1 skein

Dark green 336 – 1 skein
Light blue-green 293 – 1 skein
Dark blue-green 295 – 1 skein
Light gold 473 – 1 skein
Mid gold 695 – 1 skein
Dark gold 696 – 1 skein

Equipment
Size 7 crewel needle
Embroidery hoop or frame

Stitches Long and short stitch,
stem stitch, split back stitch,
fly stitch, open fly, Jacobean
couching and French knots.

Thread Use one strand of
crewel wool throughout.

Before you begin Prepare your
fabric then trace the outline on to
it (see below). Mount it in your
hoop or frame. Read the general
working advice on page 88.

instructions

1 Work a dark blue-green row of split back stitch around
the edge of each leaf. Fill in with long and short stitch,
starting with dark blue-green on the outside and taking
your first row of stitches over the split back stitch. The split
back stitch gives a raised effect, making it easier to produce
a straight edge with the long and short stitch. Fill in the
centre of the leaves with
light blue-green long
and short stitch.

Do not leave a gap for the centre vein since this should
be worked over the long and short stitch to give a
three-dimensional effect but do leave space for the stem.
Complete the leaves with a central vein of stem stitch in
dark green.

2 Work the stem in parallel lines of stem stitch in dark
green, dark and light gold. Begin at the dark green inner line
and when you reach the tendril carry on along its length and
then rejoin the main stem again at the base of the tendril.
(If you work in this way then the tendril will look as
though it grew rather than as
if it was stuck on later.) Work
two rows of dark green, two
rows of dark gold and one row of
light gold, adding a light gold tendril in the same way as before.
Tuck the stitches up tightly against
the leaf edges where the stem
passes under or over the leaves.

3 Now turn to the flower. The
two uppermost petals are
worked in mid coral, dark coral
and red. Start with a split back stitch
jagged edge in mid coral and then
shade in long and short stitch to the centre,
working over the split back stitch as before.

4 Work the other five petals in the same way in light, mid and dark coral, leaving a space down the centre of each. Work a row of open fly stitch in light gold down the middle of each petal and then outline it in light gold stem stitch.

5 Outline the sepals in dark green split back stitch and then fill them with fly stitch, also using dark green.

6 Cover the area of the calyx in mid gold long and short stitch. Lay a trellis of long stitches over this in red. First lay all the stitches in one direction and then lay those in the other direction on top. You will find it easier if you lay the first thread in each direction across the middle of the shape and then fill to each side rather than trying to start with a short stitch across an edge. Finally, couch down each inter-

section of the laid threads with a tiny upright cross stitch in dark blue-green.

7 Add a few dark green French knots to the top and bottom edges of the calyx to cover any slight gaps. This is a useful way of making two groups of stitching join together so that in this case the flower looks as though it grew from the stem naturally.

F I N I S H I N G   O F F

When you have finished the embroidery wash and press it carefully to remove any wrinkles (see page 91). Mount and frame it as required (see page 108).

Rose and Pansy Purse

Fabric 15in x 10in (38 x 25cm) rectangle of fine linen and another piece the same size for the back of the purse

Appleton crewel wool (yarn)
Light yellow 471 – 1 skein
Dark yellow 473 – 1 skein
Light pink 221 – 1 skein

Mid pink 222 – 1 skein
Dark pink 223 – 1 skein
Light green 332 – 1 skein
Mid green 334 – 1 skein
Dark green 336 – 1 skein
Light violet 604 – 1 skein
Dark violet 607 – 1 skein
Red 504 – 1 skein
Dark brown 588 – 1 skein

Equipment
Size 7 crewel needle
Embroidery hoop or frame

Stitches Long and short stitch, stem stitch, split back stitch, satin stitch and French knots.

Threads Use one strand of crewel wool throughout.

Before you begin Prepare your fabric then trace the outline on to it (see opposite). Mount it in your hoop or frame. Read the general working advice on page 88.

instructions

1 Work the petals of the rose in long and short stitch shaded from light, through mid to dark pink in the centre. Fill the turned-over edges at the tips with dark pink satin stitch.

2 Fill the centre of the rose with light yellow French knots around the edge and dark yellow in the middle.

3 Divide the petals with a line of dark green split back stitch and add a few short, straight stitches to the end of each line to look like sepals.

4 Work a mid green row of split back stitch around the edge of each of the four rose leaves. Fill in with a single row of long and short stitch in mid green, taking your stitches over the split back stitch. The split back stitch gives a raised effect and makes it easier to produce a straight edge with the long and short stitch.

5 Work the rosebud in long and short stitch in light green with a few dark pink stitches in the centre. Leave the dark green area at the base until you work the stems.

6   Now work the pansy. Outline the top two petals in dark violet split back stitch then fill with long and short stitch shaded from dark violet, through light violet to light yellow.

7   Work the inner parts of remaining petals in long and short stitch in dark yellow, through light yellow to dark brown at the centre. Fill the small turned-over edges with dark violet satin stitch.

8   Divide the petals with a line of dark green split back stitch and add a few short, straight stitches to the end of each line. Fill the centre of the flower with a cluster of tightly packed light yellow French knots.

9   Work a row of mid green split back stitch around the edge of the large pansy leaf. Fill it with long and short stitch shaded in mid green at the outside and light green at the centre. Stitch the small leaf in light green long and short stitch, filling it right to the centre – the leaf vein is added later on top.

10 For the pansy bud use long and short stitch worked in light violet, light yellow and mid green (see photograph, left).

11 The stems and veins are all worked in stem stitch. Refer to the photograph to place the greens, working in the direction of growth. Add the area at the base of the rosebud.

12 Turning to the ladybird, work its wing cases in red long and short stitch. Let your stitches radiate out at the top and turn in at the bottom – even on something this small it is still important. Fill the body with a few dark brown stitches and work a line between the wings using split back stitch. Make French knot spots on each side and cover the head with tightly packed French knots in dark brown. For the feelers and legs use small dark brown straight stitches.

13 Work the wings of the butterfly in long and short stitch in dark violet, light violet and a little red. Work the body in mid green. For the head work a cluster of dark brown French knots and for the feelers and legs use small dark brown straight stitches.

FINISHING OFF

When you have finished the embroidery wash and press it carefully to remove any wrinkles (see page 91). Bag tops can be hard to find in a style you like and because they vary it is impossible to provide instructions suitable for all. I found an old Bakelite bag top which was a lucky junk-shop find. Buy the bag top before you cut any shape into the fabric and I suggest that you make a bag out of calico first to test the shape before you risk your embroidery.

chapter two

Fruits and Flowers of the Forest

Fruits and flowers belong together because one is derived from the other. Fruits symbolise fertility and plenty and many of those that appear in traditional crewelwork have a fanciful nature, the design being based on the real thing but with a slightly mythical look. They are usually worked in rich, deep colours and often highly decorated. In keeping with this tradition I have chosen to feature a pineapple and pomegranate, both exotic fruit and naturally rich in colour. The pomegranate also carries with it a mythical association since it was the seeds of this fruit which Persephone ate in the underworld when she was forced there by Hades. Because she ate the fruit she must return to the underworld for a third of each year, during which time her mother Demeter mourns and the earth is turned into winter.

Fruits and Flowers Bell Pull

his richly coloured bell pull combines designs from this chapter and the previous one, showing just how easy it is to adapt designs for crewel embroidery. I traced my selected fruits and flowers and then adjusted the stems a little to make them flow through the design. I added a fifth flower for balance – the tulip in the middle. Finally, I reversed the drawing to make it look sufficiently different from the originals. If you wish you can design your own bell pull using other motifs from this book and elsewhere.

you will need

Fabric 32 x 14in (80 x 35cm) rectangle of pure linen twill

Appleton crewel wool (yarn)
Light coral 204 – 1 skein
Mid coral 205 – 1 skein
Dark coral 207 – 1 skein
Light gold 695 – 1 skein
Mid gold 475 – 1 skein
Dark gold 696 – 1 skein

Deep red 725 – 1 skein
Light mauve 933 – 1 skein
Dark mauve 934 – 1 skein
Light green 332 – 2 skein
Mid green 334 – 2 skein
Dark green 336 – 2 skein
Light blue-green 293 – 1 skein
Dark blue-green 295 – 1 skein

Equipment
Size 7 crewel needle
Size 24 tapestry needle
Embroidery frame

Stitches Split back stitch, long and short stitch, stem stitch, buttonhole stitch, detached buttonhole stitch, fly stitch, open fly stitch, straight spider's web stitch, Jacobean couching and French knots.

Threads Use one strand of crewel wool throughout.

Before you begin Prepare your fabric then trace the outline on to it (see page 96). Mount it in your frame.

instructions

the pineapple

1   Work a row of split back stitch around the edge of each leaf in the colour that you will use as the outside colour – mid green for the small leaves and the top of the large leaf and dark green for the underside of the large leaf. Fill in with long and short stitch, taking your stitches over the split back stitch. Use mid green with light green in the centre for the two small leaves and the top of the large leaf. For the underside of the large leaf use dark green with mid green in the centre. Do not leave space for the vein which is worked on top, but do leave a gap for the stem. Work a central vein of stem stitch in dark green on the underside of the large leaf and use mid green for the small leaves and the top of the large leaf. By working over the long and short stitch you will give the leaf a three-dimensional look.

2   Outline the three sepals at the base of the fruit with split back stitch using light blue-green. Fill them in with fly stitch in the same colour. For the two outer leaves at the base work dark blue-green long and short stitch to the inner line, then work buttonhole stitch in dark blue-green and edge it in mid gold stem stitch.

3   Work the edges of the pineapple plates in buttonhole stitch but with long and short ends so that you can then carry on in long and short stitch. As you stitch these shapes add spines in the same colour where required, referring to the photograph as your guide. Start with the bottom plates, edging them in dark gold and finishing them with dark mauve long and short stitch. Work the next two rows in mid gold at the edges with dark gold long and short stitch centres, leaving a gap for the French knots. Work the next row in light gold at the edge with mid gold centres. Work the top two rows all in light gold. Work the two tiny infill shapes at the very top in dark gold buttonhole stitch.

4   Pack French knots very tightly into each gap at the base of the plates. Use dark coral at the bottom, then a mix of dark and mid coral, then a mix of mid and light coral and towards the top use light coral.

5   Turn to the leaves at the top of the pineapple. Fill the two lower ones with long and short stitch, using light blue-green at the upper edge and dark blue-green at the base. Finish each leaf with a row of dark blue-green stem stitch

along the top edge which should extend out to become the tendril. As you work along the tendrils towards the tips make your stitches progressively shorter so it is easier to work around the curly ends. Work the top three leaves in the same way using dark blue-green and dark mauve long and short stitch and finishing with dark mauve stem stitch.

the carnation

6   Work a dark blue-green row of split back stitch around the edge of each leaf and fill in with long and short stitch, starting with dark blue-green on the outside and filling the centre with light blue-green. Complete with a central vein of stem stitch in dark green.

7   Work the two uppermost petals of the flower in mid coral, dark coral and deep red. Start with a split back stitch jagged edge in mid coral and then shade in long and short stitch to the centre, working over the split back stitch as before. Work the other five petals in the same way in light, mid and dark coral, leaving a space down the centre of each. Work a row of open fly stitch in light gold down the middle of each petal and then outline it in light gold stem stitch. Outline the sepals in dark green split back stitch and then fill them with fly stitch, also using dark green.

8   Cover the calyx in mid gold long and short stitch. Lay a trellis of long stitches over this in red, working first in one direction, then in the other. You will find it easier if you lay the first thread in each direction across the middle of the shape

11

12

14

16

13

15

21

18

20

19

17

and then fill to each side rather than trying to start with a short stitch across an edge. Couch down each intersection of the threads with a tiny upright cross stitch in dark blue-green. Add a few dark green French knots to the top and bottom edges of the calyx to cover any slight gaps.

the tulip

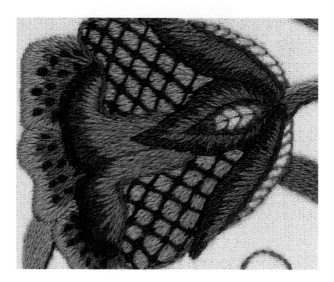

9 Work the leaves in long and short stitch in all three shades of green: light at the tops working through to dark at the base. Work the leaf undersides in light mauve. Work a row of dark green stem stitch along the edge of each leaf which will define the twist at the end and continue on as a tendril on the end of the bottom leaf. Where one leaf grows out from under another tuck your stitches under well so that no fabric shows through and the leaves look as though they are growing and not just stuck together. Work the flower stem in parallel rows of stem stitch: two rows of light green, two rows of mid green and one row of dark green.

10 Work the two outer petals in light gold long and short stitch then lay a trellis of long stitches over this in deep red. Couch down each intersection of the threads with a tiny upright cross stitch in dark mauve. Work the two central petals in mid and light coral, using buttonhole stitch to define the top edge but with long and short ends so that you can then carry on down the petals in long and short stitch. Thread a fine tapestry

needle with deep red and work a row of detached buttonhole stitch by picking up the loops of the buttonhole edge to make a second layer which stands away from the fabric.

11 Outline the top three petals in light gold split back stitch and then fill with long and short stitch shaded in light gold at the edge and dark gold towards the centre. Scatter deep red French knots over these petals. Work a light mauve stem stitch outline around the two petals with Jacobean couching.

12 Outline the outer parts of the sepals in dark green split back stitch. Fill with dark green long and short stitch at the edge with mid green to the inner line. For the middle sepal work open fly stitch in mid green down the centre with a row of dark coral stem stitch along each side. For the two outer sepals work open buttonhole stitch in place of the fly stitch so it looks like half of the fly stitch. Edge it in dark coral stem stitch on one side only.

the pomegranate

13 Work dark green split back stitch around the edge of the top two leaves and fill in with long and short stitch. Use dark green at the edge shading through mid green to light green at the centre. Add a vein of mid green stem stitch on each one. Work the lower leaf in the same way but add a mid green open fly stitch line down the centre with a row of stem stitch along each side. For the upper part of this leaf use dark and mid green long and short stitch only. Starting where the stem and the leaf cross, work a line of dark green stem stitch and continue it on as a tendril.

14 Begin the fruit with straight spider's web stitch in dark gold so that the long and short stitch worked next to it will cover the edges. Lay plenty of horizontal threads. Change to a fine tapestry needle to weave the whipping thread around the laid bars. Pack the bars tightly so that they begin to stand away from the fabric.

15 Fill the centre with light gold long and short stitch. Work clusters of French knots in mauve on top (see photograph for placement). For the outer sides of the pomegranate use long and short stitch shaded in light, mid and dark coral. Work only a few dark stitches and do not take them into the centre.

16 Turn to the three small leaves at the top and bottom of the fruit. Work a row of dark blue-green split back stitch around the outer leaves, then fill in with fly stitch in the same colour. Repeat for the central leaf but use light blue-green.

the pansy

17 Outline the small leaf in dark green split back stitch and fill with dark green long and short stitch, shading through mid green to light green at the centre. Work the large leaf, using mid and light green long and short stitch around the edges.

Work open fly stitch in mid green up the centre gap and then outline this in light mauve stem stitch.

18 Work a light coral split back stitch edge around the two uppermost petals of the pansy and then fill with long and short stitch, using light coral at the edge and working down through dark coral to light mauve at the centre.

19 Work the edges of the three lower petals in dark mauve straight spider's web stitch. Outline the inner sections of these petals in dark gold using split back stitch. Fill in with long and short stitch, starting with dark gold and shading through light gold to dark mauve. Work a line of dark coral stem stitch between the dark mauve spider's web stitch and the dark gold so that the spider's web stitch looks like petal tips which have turned over.

20 Work the sepals between the petals in mid green fly stitch, outlining them first in split back stitch and working over these stitches. Fill the centre of the flower with a tightly packed cluster of dark gold French knots and add a few French knots in dark mauve to the base of the large leaf to cover any slight gaps.

21 Use stem stitch for the stems. For the pansy work one row of light mauve, two rows of dark mauve and one row of dark gold, adding a dark gold tendril as you go. Add a small cluster of dark mauve French knots to the end of the stem to look like a cut edge. For the pomegranate work two rows of dark blue-green, two rows of light blue-green and one row of dark gold, again adding tendrils in dark gold as you go. For the carnation work two rows of dark green, two rows of mid green and one row of dark mauve. Add tendrils in dark mauve and mid green as you go. Finally, for the pineapple work two rows of dark green, two rows of mid green and one row of dark mauve.

FINISHING OFF

When you have finished the embroidery wash and press it carefully to remove any wrinkles (see page 91). To assemble it as a bell pull see page 111.

Luxurious Pillows

The pineapple has long been known as a sign of welcome and the pomegranate one of plenty so this pair of plush velvet pillows creates just the right note of welcome in a living room. These designs could easily be framed as pictures to go with the pansy and carnation from the previous chapter but I am passionate about the presentation of embroidery. Here you can see how two relatively small pieces of work can be trimmed with velvet, braids and tassels and turned into much weightier objects. I never stint on fabrics and trimmings and the more luxurious the trimmings you choose the better.

Pineapple Pillow

······································ *you will need* ······································

Fabric 10in (25cm) square of pure linen twill

Appleton crewel wool (yarn)
Light coral 205 – 1 skein
Mid coral 207 – 1 skein
Dark coral 725 – 1 skein
Light gold 695 – 1 skein

Mid gold 475 – 1 skein
Dark gold 696 – 1 skein
Light green 332 – 1 skein
Mid green 334 – 1 skein
Dark green 336 – 1 skein
Light blue-green 293 – 1 skein
Dark blue-green 295 – 1 skein
Dark mauve 934 – 1 skein

Equipment
Size 7 crewel needle
Embroidery hoop or frame

Stitches Long and short stitch, stem stitch, split back stitch, buttonhole stitch, fly stitch and French knots.

Threads Use one strand of crewel wool throughout.

Before you begin Prepare your fabric then trace the outline on to it (see below). Mount it in your hoop or frame. Read the general working advice on page 88.

instructions

1　Work a row of split back stitch around the edge of each leaf in the colour that you will use as the outside colour – mid green for the small leaves and the top of the large leaf and dark green for the underside of the large leaf. Fill in the leaves in long and short stitch, taking your stitches over the split back stitch. The split back stitch gives a raised effect and makes it easier to produce a straight edge. Use mid green with light green in the centre for the two small leaves and the top of the large leaf. For the underside of the large leaf use dark

green with mid green in the centre. Do not leave space for the vein which is worked on top, but do leave a gap for the stem.

2　Work a central line of stem stitch in dark green on the underside of the large leaf and use mid green for the small leaves and the top of the large leaf. By working over the long and short stitch you will give the leaf a three-dimensional look.

3　Outline the three sepals at the base of the fruit with split back stitch using light blue-green. Fill them in with fly stitch in the same colour.

4　For the two outer leaves at the base work dark blue-green long and short stitch to the inner line, then work buttonhole stitch in dark blue-green and edge it in mid gold stem stitch.

5　Work the edges of the pineapple plates in buttonhole stitch but with long and short ends so that you can then carry on in long and short stitch. As you stitch these shapes add spines in the same colour where required, referring to the photograph as your guide. Start with the bottom plates, edging them in dark gold and finishing them with dark mauve long and short stitch. Work the next two rows in mid gold at the edges with dark gold long and short

stitch centres, leaving a gap for the French knots. Work the next row in light gold at the edge with mid gold centres. Finally, work the top two rows in light gold.

6   Work the two tiny infill shapes at the very top in dark gold buttonhole stitch.

7   Pack French knots very tightly into each gap at the base of the plates. Use dark coral at the bottom, then a mix of dark and mid coral, then a mix of mid and light coral and towards the top use light coral.

8   Turn to the leaves at the top of the pineapple. Fill the two lower ones with long and short stitch, using light blue-green at the upper edge and dark blue-green at the bottom. Finish each leaf with a row of dark blue-green stem stitch along the top edge which should extend out to become the tendril. As you work

along the tendrils towards the tips make your stitches shorter so it is easier to work around the ends. Work the top three leaves in the same way, using dark blue-green and dark mauve long and short stitch and finishing with dark mauve stem stitch.

9   The stem is made up of parallel lines of stem stitch in dark green, dark mauve and mid green. Begin at the dark green lower line. Work two rows of dark green, one row of dark mauve and two rows of mid green. Tuck the stitches tightly up against the leaf edges where the stem passes in front of the lower leaf. Thicken the end of the stem by adding extra mid green stitches.

F I N I S H I N G   O F F

When you have finished the embroidery wash and press it carefully to remove any wrinkles (see page 91). To make up the pillow see page 112.

Pomegranate Pillow

Fabric 10in (25cm) square of
pure linen twill

Appleton crewel wool (yarn)
Light coral 204 – 1 skein
Mid coral 205 – 1 skein
Dark coral 207 – 1 skein
Light gold 695 – 1 skein
Dark gold 696 – 1 skein

Light green 332 – 1 skein
Mauve 933 – 1 skein
Mid green 334 – 1 skein
Dark green 336 – 1 skein
Light blue-green 293 – 1 skein
Dark blue-green 295 – 1 skein

Equipment
Size 7 crewel needle

Size 24 tapestry needle
Embroidery hoop or frame

Stitches Long and short stitch,
stem stitch, split back stitch,
fly stitch, open fly stitch,
straight spider's web stitch
and French knots.

Threads Use one strand of
crewel wool throughout.

Before you begin Prepare your
fabric then trace the outline on
to it (see below). Mount it in
your hoop or frame. Read the
general working advice on
page 88.

instructions

1   Work a row of dark green split back stitch around the
edge of the top two leaves. Fill in the leaves in long and short
stitch, taking your stitches over the split back stitch. The split
back stitch gives a raised effect and makes it easier to produce
a straight edge with the long and short stitch. Use dark green
at the edge shading through mid green to light green at the
centre. Do not leave space for the vein which is worked on
top. Work a central vein of mid green stem stitch to complete
each upper leaf.

2   Work the lower leaf in the same way as the other two
but add a line of mid green open fly stitch down the centre
with a row of stem stitch along each side. For the upper part
of this leaf use dark and mid green long and short stitch only.
Starting where the stem and the leaf cross,
work a line of dark green stem stitch and
continue it on as the tendril.

3   The stem is made up of parallel lines
of stem stitch in all three greens. Begin at the
dark green outer line and when you reach
each tendril carry on along it to the end and
then rejoin the main stem at the base of the
tendril. Work two rows of dark green, two
of mid green and one of light green.

4   To create the shape at the cut
end of the stem work two ovals of
dark green stem stitch filled with mid
green French knots.

5   Begin the fruit with straight spider's web
stitch in dark gold so that the long and short

stitch worked next to it will cover the edges. Lay plenty of horizontal threads. You will find it easier to change to a fine tapestry needle to weave the whipping thread around the laid bars. You can work up and down and do not worry that the first rows look a little uneven. You will need to weave more rows in the middle section than at each end – as the bars become full leave them out. Pack the bars tightly so that they begin to stand away from the fabric.

6 Fill the central area with long and short stitch in light gold. The stitches should radiate out from the top and turn in again at the bottom. Cover the entire area, then work clusters of French knots in mauve on top of the gold stitching, referring to the photograph for placement.

7 For the outer sides of the pomegranate use long and short stitch shaded in light, mid and dark coral. Work only a few dark stitches and do not take them right into the centre. As you work each colour do not finish off the thread but leave it to one side so you can add in another stitch if you want to change the colour blending as you progress.

8 Turn to the three small leaves at the top and bottom of the fruit. Work a row of dark blue-green around the edge of the outer leaves and then fill in with fly stitch in the same colour. Repeat for the central leaf but use light blue-green.

FINISHING OFF

When you have finished the embroidery wash and press it carefully to remove any wrinkles (see page 91). To make up the pillow see page 112.

Strawberry Pot

This delightful little design could be put to a host of different uses, as embroidery for clothing or tableware, for example, but I chose to mount it in the lid of this hand-turned wooden ring pot. The pot can be used to store pins, stamps or any other small items.

you will need

Fabric 8in (20cm) square of pure linen twill	Dark green 546 – 1 skein Light green 544 – 1 skein	*Stitches* Long and short stitch, stem stitch, split back stitch, fly stitch, Jacobean couching and French knots.	*Before you begin* Prepare your fabric then trace the outline on to it (see above right). Mount it in your hoop or frame. Read
Appleton crewel wool (yarn) Yellow 473 – 1 skein Red 866 – 1 skein Mauve 934 – 1 skein	*Equipment* Size 7 crewel needle Embroidery hoop or frame	*Threads* Use one strand of crewel wool throughout.	the general working advice on page 88.

instructions

1 Work a row of dark green split back stitch around the edge of each leaf. Fill in the leaves in long and short stitch, taking your stitches over the split back stitch. The split back stitch gives a raised effect and makes it easier to produce a straight edge with the long and short stitch. Use dark green at the edges with light green in the centre. Do not leave space for the vein which is worked on top. This helps to give the leaves a three-dimensional look.

6 Work the wing cases of the ladybird in red long and short stitch. Let your stitches radiate out at the top and turn in at the bottom – even on something this small it is still important. Fill the body with a few mauve stitches and work a line between the wings using split back stitch. Make French knot spots on each side and cover the head with tightly packed French knots in mauve. For the feelers work a few stem stitches and for the legs use straight stitches in mauve.

FINISHING OFF

When you have finished the embroidery wash and press it carefully to remove any wrinkles (see page 91). Mount and frame the embroidery as required. I mounted my strawberry on the lid of a turned wooden ring pot and trimmed the edge of it with a twisted cord made from red and dark green (see page 110).

2 Cover the entire strawberry with red long and short stitch. Your stitches should radiate out at the top of the fruit and turn in again at the bottom. Lay a trellis of long stitches over this in mauve. Lay all the stitches in one direction first and then lay them in the other direction. You will find it easier if you lay the first thread in each direction across the middle of the shape and then fill to each side rather than trying to start with a short stitch across an edge. Couch down each intersection of the threads with a tiny upright cross stitch in yellow.

3 Work an outline of dark green split back stitch around each of the sepals at the top the fruit. Fill them with dark green fly stitch.

4 Add a few mauve French knots where the sepals join the fruit to hide any gaps and to add textural interest.

5 Work all the stems and leaf veins in mauve stem stitch. Begin at the bottom and work in the direction of growth. Allow the main stem to run right to the tip of one leaf and then join it carefully to the main stem to work a second line. Work a second row of stem stitch in dark green on the bottom curl of the stem.

chapter three

Beasts of the Field

Many of the seventeenth-century
crewelwork scenes that have survived
today are inhabited by a race of rather
quaint and often slightly grotesque
animals. These were based on the stories
of merchants who had been to far-flung
places or sometimes copied from designs
which the merchants brought back with
them. Not surprisingly, some of the
animal figures created on this basis were
not quite as they should be, but then this
is all part of their charm.

The Lion and the Unicorn Workbox

This rather worried looking lion and his benign companion, the unicorn, were inspired by browsing through books of seventeenth-century embroideries. There are pictures of this type worked in many different embroidery techniques – stumpwork, canvaswork and very fine silk embroidery as well as crewelwork. I love the way that the embroiderers of this period did not concern themselves with perspective or the true size of the design elements relative to each other. They seemed simply to select a set of plants and creatures and assemble them as a picture, filling in the gaps with birds and insects. However, this seemingly haphazard way of working produces designs of great charm.

you will need

Fabric 20 x 16in (40 x 50cm) rectangle of pure linen twill

Appleton crewel wool (yarn)
Off-white 992 – 1 skein
Light pink 204 – 1 skein
Dark pink 205 – 1 skein
Dark coral 207 – 1 skein
Light gold 695 – 1 skein
Dark gold 696 – 1 skein

Orange 477 – 1 skein
Light mauve 605 – 1 skein
Dark mauve 606 – 1 skein
Light green 355 – 1 skein
Dark green 356 – 1 skein
Light blue-green 642 – 1 skein
Dark blue-green 644 – 1 skein
Golden brown 698 – 1 skein
Light brown 953 – 1 skein
Dark brown 955 – 1 skein

Equipment
Size 7 crewel needle
Embroidery frame

Stitches Long and short stitch, stem stitch, split back stitch, fly stitch, chain stitch, satin stitch, bullion knots and French knots.

Threads Use one strand of crewel wool throughout.

Before you begin Prepare your fabric then trace the outline on to it (see page 98). Mount it in your frame. Read the general working advice on page 88.

instructions

the oak tree

1   Work the leaves of the tree in light and dark green or light and dark blue-green, placing the colours where you like or referring to the photograph to make an exact copy. Outline each leaf in your chosen colour in split back stitch and then fill in with satin stitch, working over the split back stitch to give a raised outline and stitching from the outside of the leaf to a central vein. You will need to overlap your stitches at the centre to work your way around the tip of the leaf.

2   Work the nuts of the acorns in light gold satin stitch with a split back stitch outline in the same way as the leaves. Loosely cover the cups with golden brown French knots and then fill to give a close cover with orange French knots.

3   Work the roots, trunk, branches and leaf veins so that they run into each other using golden brown and light and dark brown stem stitch. Begin at the bottom of the roots and stitch right up through the trunk, along a branch and out to the end of a leaf vein, then return to the base of the tree for the next row. Work two or three rows of each colour, beginning at the left side of the trunk with dark brown. You will need to add some extra short rows to fill out the bottom of the trunk – use the photograph to help you and work the rows close together so that no fabric shows through.

4   Work the grass at the base of the tree in light and dark green long and short stitch. Begin the stitching in the spaces between the roots in light green and allow your stitches to radiate out parallel to the roots. When you are roughly level with the ends of the roots change colour to dark green.

5   Work the stems and leaves of the little flowers at the base of the tree in dark green stem stitch and add clusters of French knots to make flowers in dark mauve or dark pink.

the lion

6   Work the face of the lion in dark gold long and short stitch. Begin the body at the outside of the mane in dark gold

long and short stitch, taking care with the direction of the stitches – they should radiate from around the lion's neck. Complete the body, legs and tail in long and short stitch, following the stitch direction already set.

7   Work the mane in bullion knots using golden brown and light gold. Begin at the outside edge and work inwards, making the bullion knots overlap each other and radiate out from the face. Mix the two colours as you work.

8   Outline the body with dark brown stem stitch. Add a 'tassel' to the end of the tail using dark gold and light gold straight stitches. Then work three dark brown French knots for each eye and work just a few small straight stitches for the nose and mouth.

the unicorn

9 Work the head, body, legs and tail of the unicorn in off-white long and short stitch, taking care with the stitch directions in the same way as for the lion. Work the mane, beard and forelock in golden brown bullion knots and add a cluster to the end of the tail. Work dark brown hooves in satin stitch.

10 Outline the head and body in light brown stem stitch. Stitch the horn in light brown long and short stitch and put in the eye with three French knots.

the landscape and flowers

11 The contours of the landscape are made with rows of chain stitch. Follow the lines in light blue-green and then add close lines below it in dark blue-green, dark green and light green. Work tightly up against the feet and leaves as you reach them to avoid leaving any gaps. Add little flowers at the feet of the lion and unicorn worked in the same way as the ones at the foot of the tree.

12 Outline the petals of the rose with light pink split back stitch and work a row of long and short stitch around the flower. Complete the petals with dark coral long and short stitch. Add a cluster of light gold French knots to the centre of the flower and make one long-armed French knot on each petal.

13 Outline the rose leaves in light green split back stitch and then fill with matching long and short stitch. Work the stems in dark green stem stitch and add a few light blue-green straight stitches to the base of the plant.

14 Outline the top two petals of the pansy in light mauve split back stitch and then fill with long and short stitch. Outline the three lower petals in orange split back stitch and then fill with one row of orange long and short stitch before completing in light gold. Work three dark brown French knots at the centre. Add a few straight stitches in dark green between the petals for the sepals.

15 Outline the leaves in light green split back stitch and then fill with satin stitch, turning the stitch direction at the tips of the leaves. Work stems and veins in dark green stem stitch and add a cluster of French knots around the base of the plant.

the birds and fruit branches

16 For the leaves of the fruit branches use dark blue-green or dark green and copy the colouring in the photograph or use your own mix. Outline them in split back stitch and then fill with fly stitch. For the fruits use light pink long and short stitch with dark pink French knots or dark pink long and short stitch with light pink French knots. Work the leaf stems in dark brown stem stitch and the fruit stems in golden brown stem stitch. Add two French knots to the base of each leaf or fruit in the same colour as the stem to join them on. Work the branches in golden brown long and short stitch.

17 Outline the lower edge of the wing of the bird on the right in dark mauve split back stitch and work a row of long and short stitch over it. Complete the wing in light mauve.

Work the head and body in long and short stitch, starting at the head with light gold and shading through dark coral to orange. Add a dark coral tail and work a row of French knots where the wing and body meet. Work the legs in dark brown stem stitch and make tiny feet with straight stitches. Use long and short stitch for the beak and add a French knot eye.

18 Outline the lower edge of the wing of the bird on the left in orange split back stitch and fill the lower wing with satin stitch. Outline the upper wing edge with light gold split back stitch and fill with long and short stitch. Work the head and body in long and short stitch, beginning at the head end with light mauve and shading to dark mauve. Outline the outer tail feathers with light gold and the central one with orange split back stitch and then complete these feathers with fly stitch. Add a dark coral beak in long and short stitch with a dark brown straight stitch to mark the mouth. Finally, give the bird a little foot using dark brown straight stitches.

the snail and insects

19 Work the snail shell in dark coral long and short stitch and the body in light gold. Outline the snail in dark brown stem stitch and add feelers with a French knot at the ends.

20 Cover the body of the ladybird in dark coral long and short stitch and add a dark brown under body. Work three dark

brown French knots on each side, on top of the dark coral, and cover the head with tightly packed French knots. Add tiny straight stitches for legs and feelers, still using dark brown.

21 Outline the top wings of the butterfly on the left with dark mauve split back stitch. Work a row of long and short stitch and then complete the wings in dark coral. Work the lower body (abdomen) in light gold and the upper body (thorax) in dark brown long and short stitch. Outline the abdomen in dark brown stem stitch, adding veins with straight stitches. Work a tightly packed cluster of dark brown French knots for the head and add stem stitch legs and feelers.

22 Outline the wings of the butterfly on the right with dark pink split back stitch and work a row of long and short stitch. Fill the wings with further rows of light gold and dark coral and add a few dark coral French knots on the light gold of the top wing. Work the abdomen in dark coral long and short stitch and add light gold veins. Fill the thorax with light brown long and short stitch and the head with dark brown. Work dark brown stem stitch feelers with a French knot at their ends and add tiny straight stitches for legs.

FINISHING OFF

When you have finished the embroidery wash and press it carefully to remove any wrinkles (see page 91). I set my embroidery on the top of an oak workbox and piped the edge with green velvet but you can mount and frame your finished piece as desired.

Insect Accessories

These shiny insects were inspired by all the little creatures that can be seen flying about in the backgrounds of Tudor embroideries. They were often only there to cover flaws in the fabric and, at first glance, you don't notice them. Look a little longer and suddenly you see a host of tiny creatures, often quite comical, with funny little faces and usually out of proportion but all works of art in their own right. I have taken a selection to make a very special set of needlework accessories worked in silk thread on silk fabric.

Dragonfly Needlecase

you will need

Fabric 12 x 8in (30 x 20cm) piece of silk dupion and another the same size for lining

Caron collection Soie Cristale
Yellow 4003 – 1 skein
Light green 5006 – 1 skein
Mid green 5004 – 1 skein
Dark green 5002 – 1 skein
Light purple 6013 – 1 skein
Dark purple 6021 – 1 skein

Kreinik Metallics very fine #4 braid
Colour 205C

Stranded cotton
Black DMC 310/Anchor 403

Equipment
Size 7 crewel needle
Size 24 tapestry needle
Embroidery hoop or frame

Stitches Long and short stitch, split back stitch, straight spider's web stitch, satin stitch, Jacobean couching, couching and French knots.

Threads One skein of each colour should be sufficient to make all three of the insects in this group. Use two strands of silk throughout or one strand

of gold braid with one strand of stranded cotton for couching.

Before you begin Prepare your fabric then trace the outline on to it (see below). Mount it in your hoop or frame. Read the general working advice on page 88.

instructions

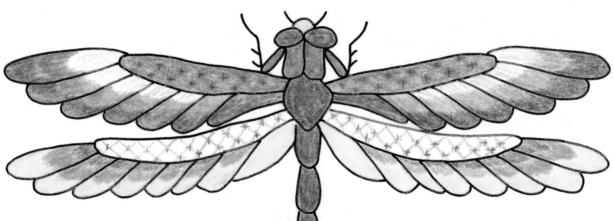

1 Work the feathery sections of the wings first. Outline the upper wings in dark purple split backstitch, then work a row of long and short stitch in dark purple along the lower edge, taking your stitches over the split back stitch. The split back stitch gives a raised effect and makes it easier to produce a straight edge with the long and short stitch. Fill the innermost sections with dark purple. Complete this section of the upper wings in long and short stitch with mid green and light green. Work the feathery sections of the lower wings in the same way, using yellow split back stitch and yellow long and short stitch followed by mid green and light purple long and short stitch. Use the photograph as a guide.

2 The top section of each wing is worked in long and short stitch covered with Jacobean couching. First work the upper

wings in dark green long and short stitch and the lower wings in light green long and short stitch. Lay your trellis of long stitches on top, using yellow for the upper wings and mid green for the lower ones. Lay all the stitches in one direction first and then in the other direction. You will find it easier if you lay the first thread in each direction across the middle of the shape and then fill to each side rather than trying to start with a short stitch across an edge. Couch down each intersection of the threads with a tiny upright cross stitch, using dark purple for the upper wings and light purple for the lower ones.

3 For the abdomen outline each section with dark purple split back stitch. Complete each section with one row of dark purple and one row of light purple long and short stitch.

4   Cover the body (thorax) with tightly packed dark purple French knots and then squeeze in a few yellow French knots as shown above.

5   The lower head is worked in dark green straight spider's web stitch. Work two sections, one right and one left so that there is a division down the centre. Lay plenty of horizontal threads. You will find it easier to change to a fine tapestry needle to weave the whipping thread around the laid bars. You can work up and down and do not worry that the first rows look uneven. You will need to weave more rows in the middle section than at each end – as the bars become full leave them out. Pack the bars tightly so that they begin to stand away from the fabric.

6   Work the top of each leg in tiny satin stitch using dark green. The lower leg will be added later.

7   Outline each eye in dark purple split back stitch and then cover it in satin stitch. Fill the remaining head section between the eyes with tightly packed yellow French knots.

8   When you have finished all the silk stitching outline the whole piece with gold braid couched down with black stranded cotton. You will need two needles, one for the braid and one to couch it down. Begin on the feathery sections of the wings. Bring the gold braid up through the silk at the tip and take it down at the other side of the section. Adjust the length of the braid to fit the shape and then couch it down with tiny stitches about ⅛in (3mm) apart, pulling the couching stitches quite tightly so they almost disappear. Surround each part of the insect, using the photograph as a guide. Add feet, feelers and pincers as you go. You will find that it helps if you work your couching stitches closer together as you work round curves – you can spread them out slightly on straight sections.

F I N I S H I N G   O F F

When you have finished the embroidery wash and press it carefully to remove any wrinkles (see page 91). To assemble the embroidery as a needlecase refer to the instructions on page 113.

Beetle Pincushion

Fabric 8in (20cm) square of pale gold silk dupion

Caron collection Soie Cristale
Dark green 5002 – 1 skein
Purple 6021 – 1 skein
Rust 3061 – 1 skein

Kreinik Metallics very fine #4 braid
Colour 002V

Stranded cotton
Old gold DMC 680/Anchor 901

Equipment
Size 7 crewel needle
Size 24 tapestry needle
Embroidery hoop or frame
Wooden-based pincushion
with a 3in (7.5cm) diameter
pad

Stitches Long and short stitch, split back stitch, straight spider's web stitch, satin stitch, Jacobean couching, couching, chain stitch and French knots.

Threads One skein of each colour should be sufficient to make all three of the insects in this group. Use two strands of silk throughout or one strand of gold braid with one strand of stranded cotton for couching.

Before you begin Prepare your fabric then trace the outline on to it (see opposite). Mount it in your hoop or frame. Read the general working advice on page 88.

instructions

1 Cover each of the wing cases with rust long and short stitch so that the stitches run from top to bottom.

2 Work the upper body in dark green straight spider's web stitch. Lay plenty of vertical threads. You will find it easier to change to a fine tapestry needle to weave the whipping thread around the laid bars. You can work forwards and backwards and do not worry that the first rows look uneven. Pack the bars tightly so that they begin to stand away from the fabric.

50

3 Outline the head in rust split back stitch and then cover it in rust satin stitch. The eyes are clusters of three purple French knots; work these closely together.

4 Work the two upper parts of each leg in tiny purple satin stitch. The lower leg will be added later.

5 Fill the two under body sections between the wing cases with tightly packed French knots, again using purple.

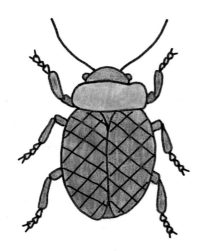

6 The wing cases are covered with gold Jacobean couching held down with purple. Lay a trellis of long gold stitches over the area. Lay all the stitches in one direction first and then in the other direction. You will find it easier if you lay the first thread in each direction across the middle of the shape and then fill to each side rather than trying to start with a short stitch across an edge. Couch down each intersection of the threads with a tiny upright cross stitch in purple.

7 When you have finished all the silk stitching outline the whole piece with gold braid couched down with old gold stranded cotton. You will need two needles, one for the braid and one to couch it down. Begin with the sections of the lower body and wing cases, bringing the gold braid up through the silk at the bottom tip of one section and taking it down at the same point. Adjust the length of the braid to fit the shape and then couch it down with tiny

stitches about ⅛in(3mm) apart, pulling the couching stitches quite tightly so they almost disappear. Surround each part of the insect using the photograph as a guide. You will find that it helps if you work your couching stitches closer together as you work round curves – you can spread them out slightly on straight sections.

8 For the lower legs work three gold braid chain stitches, holding down the last stitch with two small straight stitches.

9 The feelers are double width so make a long loop of gold braid and couch both strands side by side.

F I N I S H I N G   O F F

When you have finished the embroidery wash and press it carefully to remove any wrinkles (see page 91). Mount it on the pincushion base following the manufacturer's instructions.

Bee Scissors Keeper

Fabric 6in (15cm) square of pale green silk dupion and another piece the same size for backing

Caron collection Soie Cristale
Yellow 4003 – 1 skein
Rust 3061 – 1 skein
Light green 5006 – 1 skein
Purple 6021 – 1 skein

Kreinik Metallics very fine #4 braid
Colour 002V

Stranded cotton
Old gold DMC 680/Anchor 901

Equipment
Size 7 crewel needle
Embroidery hoop or frame

Stitches Long and short stitch, split back stitch, satin stitch, Jacobean couching, couching, chain stitch and French knots.

Threads One skein of each colour should be sufficient to make all three of the insects in this group. Use two strands of silk throughout or one

strand of gold braid with one strand of stranded cotton for couching.

Before you begin Prepare your fabric then trace the outline on to it (see below). Mount it in your hoop or frame. Read the general working advice on page 88.

instructions

1 Cover each wing with long and short stitch worked in light green. The stitches should run lengthways along the wings as indicated in the line drawing.

2 Cover the upper body (thorax) with rust long and short stitch. Cover the lower body (abdomen) with tightly packed French knots, alternating rust and yellow stripes and beginning with rust at the top.

3 Work the two upper parts of each leg in tiny rust satin stitch, packing your stitches really close together.

4 Outline the head with purple split back stitch and cover with satin stitch, taking your stitches over the split back stitch for a raised effect. The split back stitch also helps ensure you make a neat edge with the satin stitch.

5 The thorax is covered with gold Jacobean couching held down with yellow. Lay a trellis of long gold stitches over the area. Lay all the stitches in one direction first and then in the other direction. You will find it easier if you lay the first thread in each direction across the middle of the shape and then fill to each side rather than trying to start with a short stitch across an edge. Couch down each intersection of the threads with a tiny upright cross stitch in yellow.

6 When you have finished all the silk stitching outline the wings with gold braid couched down with old gold stranded cotton. You will need two needles, one for the braid and one to couch it down. Begin with the whole wing, bringing the

gold braid up through the silk at the base of the wing and taking it down at the same point opposite. Adjust the length of the braid to fit the shape and then couch it down with tiny stitches about ⅛in(3mm) apart, pulling the couching stitches quite tightly so they almost disappear. Surround each wing and then add the veins using the photograph as a guide. You will find that it helps if you work your couching stitches closer together as you work round curves – you can spread them out slightly on straight sections. Couch around the leg sections and make the feelers in the same way.

7 For the lower legs work two gold braid chain stitches, holding down the last stitch with two very small straight stitches.

F I N I S H I N G   O F F

When you have finished the embroidery wash and press it carefully to remove any wrinkles (see page 91). To assemble the scissors keeper refer to the instructions on page 114.

chapter four

Birds of Paradise

The splendid plumage of brightly coloured
birds lends itself particularly well to
interpretation in crewelwork, so it is
perhaps no surprise that they can often be
seen flying through the landscapes of
Tudor embroideries or resting on a branch
or beside a tree. They range from rather
exotic peacocks, parrots and swans to more
commonly seen small garden birds as well
as birds of the imagination. Few of them
are true to life and it is obvious that the
embroiderer let her creativity flourish
when it came to deciding on texture and
colour. You can do the same, choosing your
own colours for the birds in this chapter
and even experimenting with
different stitches if you wish.

Parrot Waistcoat

I love the gentle, rich colours and distinctive designs of traditional crewel embroidery but I was determined to include something more modern with strong, bright colours. This is why I designed my parrot. He is worked in bright stranded cottons on petrol blue silk dupion. He sits on the back of a waistcoat with his exotic tail feathers hanging low but he would also look wonderful framed as a picture.

you will need

Fabric Silk suitable for your waistcoat or a 20 x 30in (50 x 75cm) rectangle of petrol blue silk dupion if you wish to frame the design

DMC stranded cotton
Light yellow 725 – 1 skein
Dark yellow 783 – 1 skein
Light red 351 – 1 skein
Mid red 349 – 1 skein
Dark red 3777 – 1 skein
Purple 550 – 1 skein
Mauve 3726 – 1 skein
Maroon 902 – 1 skein
Light green 471 – 1 skein
Mid green 470 – 1 skein

Dark green 937 – 1 skein
Light brown 869 – 1 skein
Mid brown 801 – 1 skein
Dark brown 838 – 1 skein

Beads
Two small black ones for eyes

Equipment
Size 7 crewel needle
Size 24 tapestry needle
Embroidery frame

Stitches Split back stitch, long and short stitch, stem stitch, buttonhole stitch, fly stitch, open fly stitch, chain stitch, satin stitch, straight spider's web stitch, Jacobean couching, bullion knots and French knots.

Threads Use two strands of stranded cotton throughout.

Before you begin To make a waistcoat you will need to purchase a dressmakers' paper pattern and then adapt it by cutting a longer back to take the tail. I stitched the parrot in the middle of a piece of silk larger that the waistcoat back in each dimension but I suggest that you test your pattern in calico before you embroider and cut your silk. Then you can draw the parrot on the back of this test piece to place him before you start the silk one. Prepare your fabric then trace the outline on to it (see page 100). Mount it in your frame. Read the general working advice on page 88. The direction of your stitching is particularly important in many places on the parrot. Take care and refer to the photograph to help you.

instructions

1 Outline the lower edges of the beak with mid red split back stitch. Start filling in the beak with a row of mid red long and short stitch, taking your stitches over the split back stitch. The split back stitch gives a raised effect and makes it easier to produce a straight edge with the long and short stitch. Complete the beak in light red long and short stitch. Next outline the area below the beak in purple split back stitch and then cover the two sides in mid red satin stitch.

2 Outline the top of the head in light green split back stitch and then work a row of long and short stitch over it.

Work a second row in mid green and then fill the two sides with dark green. Work a row of French knots in dark green over the bridge of the beak to add texture.

3 Fill the sides of the face with light yellow long and short stitch. These areas are covered with dark green Jacobean couching held down with purple. Lay a trellis of long stitches over the light yellow in dark green. Lay all the stitches in one direction first and then lay those in the other direction on top. You will find it easier if you lay the first thread in each direction across the middle of the shape and then fill to each side rather than trying to start with a short stitch across an edge. Couch down each intersection of the threads with a tiny upright cross stitch in purple.

4 The neck is worked in long and short stitch running into French knots. Work a row of long and short stitch in mauve all around the lower face and then fill with extra rows at the front of the bird. Add a few long stitches in maroon amongst the mauve and then finish off the front of the neck in maroon. Complete the rest of the neck with tightly packed French knots. First scatter the area with purple ones and then fill in with maroon and then mauve.

5 Outline the four feathers below the back of the neck in mauve split back stitch and then fill them with fly stitch.

6 Most of the remaining feathers have a buttonhole stitch edge with long and short ends and are then filled with shaded

long and short stitch. Working downwards, stitch two in maroon at the top, then four in dark red, then a row with dark red edges filled in mid red, then a row with mid red edges filled in light red, then with light red edges filled in dark yellow and then with dark yellow edges filled in light yellow.

7 On the right-hand side of the bird work one mid red, two light red and three dark yellow feathers in fly stitch, outlined with split back stitch first.

8 For the two green feathers on the left first work outlines in dark green buttonhole stitch then fill with mid green. Work the other feathers in this row with dark green shaded through mid green to light green.

9 Work the top three tail feathers with dark red buttonhole stitch edges and dark red, then mid red, long and short stitch

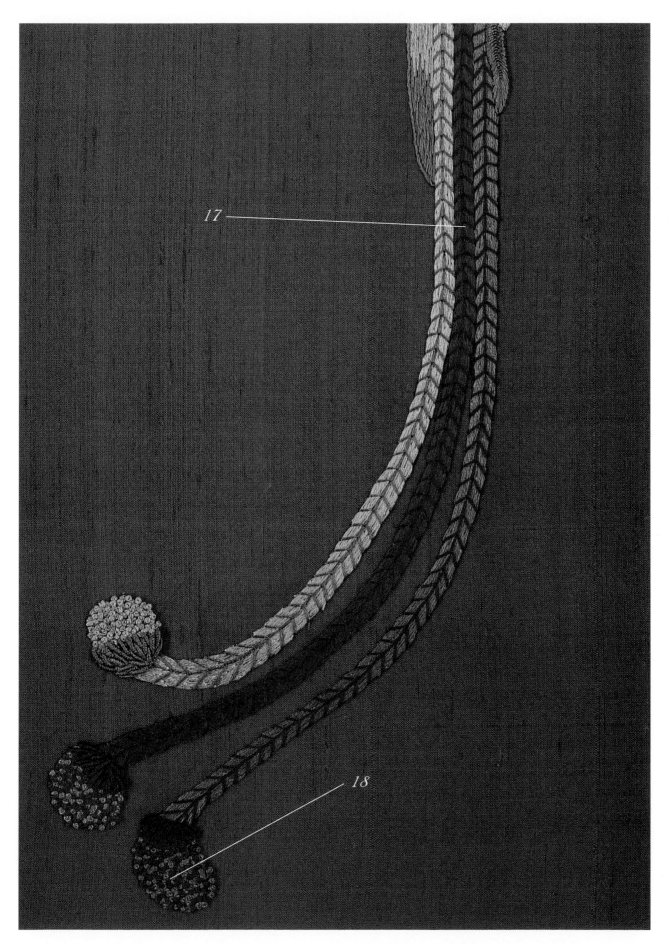

filling. For the front red feather beneath them work a mid red edge with light red long and short stitch.

10 The row of three feathers beside and beneath this one are worked in fly stitch. First outline the red feather at the front in light red split backstitch and fill with fly stitch. Repeat for the centre feather but use dark yellow, then use light yellow for the feather on the right. Work the three feathers below the light yellow one in the same way, using light green, mid green and dark green.

11 Work the long green feather at the front of the tail in long and short stitch, starting with dark green at the tip and shading to mid green and then light green further up. Outline the front of this feather in dark green stem stitch.

12 Now return to the wing. The feathers at the back under the green ones are worked in rows of chain stitch placed close together. Work them all from top to bottom, alternating lines of maroon and purple.

13 The wing tips are worked completely in long and short stitch. Begin with maroon at the ends and shade through dark red, mid red, light red and dark yellow to light yellow at the top. The second wing tip only gets as far as mid red before it disappears behind the first one.

14 Turn to the bird's stomach feathers. Work these in purple long and short stitch, then add random dark red stitches.

15 Work the foot in dark brown straight spider's web stitch. Work it in two sections: the long claws which sit over the branch first and then the leg behind. Lay plenty of vertical threads. You will find it easier to change to a fine tapestry needle to weave the whipping thread around the laid bars. You can work up and down and do not worry that the first rows look uneven. You will need to weave more rows in the middle section than at each end – as the bars become full leave them out. Pack the bars tightly so that they begin to stand away from the fabric. Complete the foot with two maroon nails in long and short stitch.

16 Using light brown cover the branch with long and short stitch, starting at one end and working up and down across the width of the branch. Add randomly spaced mid brown bullion knots on top to provide texture and colour variation.

17 Returning to the tail, work the long feathers in long and short stitch. For the front one use dark yellow, for the middle one use mid red and for the back one use mauve. Beginning at the bottom, work up each feather in open fly stitch on top of the long and short stitch. You will find that this open fly stitch separates each feather. Work this stitch in dark green fly stitch over the yellow feather, in maroon fly stitch over the red feather and in purple over the mauve feather.

18 Work French knots and bullion knots at the end of each tail feather. Start with the yellow feather, scattering the area with dark yellow French knots and then packing tightly with mid green. Overlap the French knots with lots of dark green bullion knots. Begin stitching the bullion knots next to the French knots and gradually build up until you reach the end of the long feathers. For the red feather use mid and light red French knots with maroon bullion knots. For the mauve feather use dark red and mauve French knots with purple bullion knots.

19 Finally, sew on a black bead for each eye. (I used two black glass-headed pins to try out the positions for the eyes before sewing on the beads.) Work two maroon bullion knots around each bead, one above it and the other below it, to give him eyelids.

F I N I S H I N G O F F

When you have finished the embroidery wash and press it carefully to remove any wrinkles (see page 91). Frame your design or make it up into a waistcoat following the pattern manufacturer's instructions. I worked my parrot on a piece of fabric larger than the back of the waistcoat in each dimension. Then I laid the back pattern piece over the parrot and added a semi-circle that fitted between the two darts on the waistcoat back to accommodate the tail. To make my fronts I stitched strips of red, yellow and blue silk together to make a large piece and then cut the pattern out of this.

Hardwick Birds

Hardwick Hall in Derbyshire houses a famous collection of sixteenth and seventeenth century textiles. The Countess of Shrewsbury, better known as Bess of Hardwick, had the house built in the 1590s and filled it with a vast collection of needlework and furnishings. These birds are based on a set of panels at Hardwick where they appear surrounded by blue velvet strapwork. The panels were painted on white velvet and then embroidered to embellish the painting. I have taken the images and embroidered them and then presented them in covered mounts and decorative frames.

Hardwick Swan

Fabric 10in (25cm) square of pure linen twill

Appleton crewel wool (yarn)
Off-white 992 – 1 skein
Dark pink 206 – 1 skein
Mid gold 695 – 1 skein
Dark gold 696 – 1 skein
Light green 332 – 1 skein

Mid green 334 – 1 skein
Dark green 336 – 1 skein
Light brown 952 – 1 skein
Dark brown 955 – 1 skein

Equipment
Size 7 crewel needle
Embroidery hoop or frame

Stitches Long and short stitch, split back stitch, satin stitch, stem stitch, chain stitch and French knots.

Threads One skein of each colour is sufficient to make all three birds. Use one strand of crewel wool throughout.

Before you begin Prepare your fabric then trace the outline on to it (see below). Mount it in your hoop or frame. Read the general working advice on page 88.

instructions

1   Begin at the wing edge. Work in off-white satin stitch between the layers, taking care with the direction of your stitches. The top layer of the wing is worked in long and short stitch. Finish off your thread here – your stitches will join in with the neck later (see step 2).

2   Turn to the head and work in off-white long and short stitch. Fill the head, neck and body, including the tail, taking great care with the direction of your stitches which should run parallel to those on the wing. Join in the wing as you reach it, using the photograph opposite as a guide.

3   Work the beak in mid gold long and short stitch. Next make a dark brown French knot eye.

4   Work the legs in dark gold and the feet in mid gold long and short stitch.

5   Now outline the whole bird in stem stitch. For the body and wing use light brown and for the legs, feet and beak use dark brown. Add toes to the feet with straight stitches.

6   Fill the leaves in long and short stitch, using light green at the tips and mid green at the bottom. Use the photograph to place the greens, working from the leaf tips downwards.

7   Cover the bulrush heads with French knots in dark pink and fill the gaps with light brown, packing the knots tightly to raise the shape. Work the stems in dark green stem stitch.

8   Work the contours of the land with rows of chain stitch. Follow the line in dark green and then add close lines below in mid and light green. Work tightly up against the feet and leaves as you reach them to prevent leaving any gaps.

F I N I S H I N G   O F F

When you have finished the embroidery wash and press it carefully to remove any wrinkles (see page 91). Mount and frame the design as required (see page 108). I used bright silk dupion to cover the mount and then added a cord trim made from a space-dyed thread. The silk mount really enhances this small piece — I never scrimp on trimmings and always like to take a little time to think how I can embellish the embroidery rather than just putting it straight in a frame.

Hardwick Ostrich

Fabric 10in (25cm) square of
pure linen twill

Appleton crewel wool (yarn)
Off-white 992 – 1 skein
Light pink 204 – 1 skein
Dark pink 206 – 1 skein
Red 226 – 1 skein

Light gold 692 – 1 skein
Mid gold 695 – 1 skein
Mauve 933 – 1 skein
Light green 332 – 1 skein
Mid green 334 – 1 skein
Dark green 336 – 1 skein
Light brown 952 – 1 skein
Dark brown 955 – 1 skein

Equipment
Size 7 crewel needle
Embroidery hoop or frame

Stitches Long and short stitch,
stem stitch, split back stitch,
satin stitch, chain stitch, fly
stitch and French knots.

Threads Use one strand of
crewel wool throughout.

Before you begin Prepare your
fabric then trace the outline on
to it (see below). Mount it in your
hoop or frame. Read the general
working advice on page 88.

instructions

1   Begin at the edge of the wing. Work a row of split back stitch in dark brown along the edge. Then work a row of dark brown long and short stitch along this edge, taking your stitches over the split back stitch. The split back stitch gives a raised effect and makes it easier to produce a straight edge with the long and short stitch. Complete the wing with a row of light brown and a row of light pink long and short stitch,

adding some extra light pink towards the top of the wing to shape it. Fill the rest of the wing with light gold. Finish off your thread here – your stitches will join in with the neck later.

2   Starting at the head end of the neck, work in light gold long and short stitch. Fill the neck, body and thighs, taking great care with the direction of your stitches. Join in the wing as you reach it, using the photograph as a guide. Finish the legs in light pink and the feet in dark pink.

3   Outline the two long tail feathers in split back stitch using dark pink wool (yarn) and then fill them with fly stitch in the same colour.

4   Work the beak in dark brown long and short stitch and complete the head in light gold and light pink. Make a dark brown French knot eye.

5   Outline the bird in light brown stem stitch and the feet in dark brown.

6   Work the snake in mid gold long and short stitch, taking care with the direction of your stitches – they should follow the shape of its body. Make dark green stripes and give him a forked tongue with straight stitches.

7   Work the little flying insect in long and short stitch. Use mauve and mid gold on the upper wings, and mid gold

and dark pink on the lower wing. Work the abdomen in dark brown, still using long and short stitch. Work the upper body (thorax) and head in dark brown French knots and the legs and feelers in dark brown stem stitch.

8 Outline the lower leaves of the strawberry plant in mid green split back stitch and the upper ones in light green. Then fill the leaves with matching fly stitch. Add a few French knots where the leaves meet. For the strawberry use red long and short stitch with light green on the sepals. Add a few mid green French knots where the sepals and strawberry join and then scatter some mid gold knots over the fruit. Work the petals of the tiny flower in off-white satin stitch, separating them with single long stitches in mid green. Fill the centre with a cluster of mid gold French knots. For the small fruit work a cluster of red French knots, adding sepals in light green long and short stitch.

9 The contours of the land are rows of chain stitch. Follow the line in dark green and then add close lines below in mid and light green. Work tightly up against the feet and leaves as you reach them to avoid leaving any gaps.

F I N I S H I N G   O F F

When you have finished the embroidery wash and press it carefully to remove any wrinkles (see page 91). Mount and frame the design as required (see page 108). I used bright silk dupion to cover the mount and then added a cord trim made from a space-dyed thread. The silk mount really enhances this small piece — I never scrimp on trimmings and always like to take a little time to think how I can embellish the embroidery rather than just putting it straight in a frame.

Pink Hardwick Bird

you will need

Fabric 10in (25cm) square of pure linen twill

Appleton crewel wool (yarn)
Off-white 992 – 1 skein
Light pink 204 – 1 skein
Dark pink 206 – 1 skein
Red 226 – 1 skein
Mauve 933 – 1 skein

Light gold 692 – 1 skein
Mid gold 695 – 1 skein
Dark gold 696 – 1 skein
Light green 332 – 1 skein
Mid green 334 – 1 skein
Dark green 336 – 1 skein
Light brown 952 – 1 skein
Dark brown 955 – 1 skein

Equipment
Size 7 crewel needle
Embroidery hoop or frame

Stitches Long and short stitch, stem stitch, split back stitch, satin stitch, chain stitch, fly stitch and French knots.

Threads Use one strand of crewel wool throughout.

Before you begin Prepare your fabric then trace the outline on to it (see below). Mount it in your hoop or frame. Read the general working advice on page 88.

instructions

1 Outline the three outer tips of each wing in mauve split back stitch. Work a row of mauve long and short stitch on these tips, taking your stitches over the split back stitch. The split back stitch gives a raised effect and makes it easier to produce a straight edge with the long and short stitch.

2 Work a dark pink split back stitch outline along the inner wing edge and then work a row of long and short stitch across the whole wing in the same colour. Fill the rest of the wing above with light pink long and short stitch. Finish off your thread here – your stitches will join in with the body later.

3 Beginning at the tail tips, work in long and short stitch to fill the body and head up to the beak. Start with mauve and change to dark pink and then light pink, using the photograph as a guide. Use off-white for the front of the bird. Take care with the direction of your stitches and join in the wing as you work.

4 Work the legs in light brown long and short stitch and the feet in dark gold.

5 Outline the bird in light brown stem stitch except the feet, legs and beak which should be outlined in mauve. Use stem stitch to divide the head from the body at the same time.

6 Work the wings of the left-hand insect in red and dark pink long and short stitch, referring to the photograph as a guide. Outline the lower body (abdomen) in light brown stem stitch and fill with light gold long and short stitch. For the upper body (thorax) use mauve long and short stitch, adding French knots where the wings join. Fill the head with French knots too. Work the legs and feelers in mauve stem stitch.

7 Work the wings of the top insect with mid gold and mauve long and short stitch. Outline the abdomen in dark brown stem stitch and fill with dark gold long and short stitch. For the thorax work tightly packed French knots in dark brown. Work the head in dark brown satin stitch and the legs and feelers in dark brown stem stitch.

8 For the right-hand insect work the wings in mauve and dark gold long and short stitch. Work the abdomen in dark gold and fill the thorax with tightly packed dark brown French knots. Fill the head with dark brown satin stitch and work the legs and feelers in dark brown stem stitch.

9 Outline the leaves of the little flower in light green split back stitch and then fill with matching satin stitch. Work the stems and veins in mid green stem stitch. Add a cluster of mid green French knots to the centre of the lower leaves for texture and to fill any gaps. The petals of the flower are mid gold. Work

them in satin stitch and add a cluster of red French knots in the centre. Work the flower bud in light green and mid gold, adding small straight stitches where the stem joins the leaves.

10 The contours of the land are rows of chain stitch. Follow the line in dark green and then add close lines below in mid and light green. Work tightly up against the feet and leaves as you reach them to avoid leaving any gaps.

FINISHING OFF

When you have finished the embroidery wash and press it carefully to remove any wrinkles (see page 91). Mount and frame the design as required (see page 108). I used bright silk dupion to cover the mount and then added a cord trim made from a space-dyed thread. I never scrimp on trimmings and always take time to think how I can embellish my embroidery rather than just putting it straight in a frame.

chapter five

Tree of Life

The legend of the Tree of Life can be
traced back in biblical history to the
Garden of Eden since it was the tree which
bore the apple that Eve plucked for Adam.
It has also been linked to the cross on
which Christ died, thereby marking the
start of our downfall but also the fruition of
Christ's labours for our salvation.
In fact the legend can be traced back in
other cultures and religions too — examples
can be found in Persian rugs and decorative panels dating from an early time. It's
not surprising then that the tree has been
a popular symbol in crewelwork
from the beginning.

Tree of Life Fire Screen

*T*he design for my fire screen is inspired by numerous examples of the Tree of Life legend found throughout seventeenth-century embroideries. These were stitched in canvaswork, cross stitch and stumpwork, as well as crewel embroidery, and Adam and Eve are sometimes featured also. The tree, with large leaves and swollen fruits, stands on undulating hillocks symbolic of the Garden of Paradise. I love the freedom in design that appears in all the embroideries of this period. No one seemed at all concerned with proportion – the tree would fall over if the fruits were really so large and the insects would be rather dangerous. Here I have used the strong, rich colours which I like, but you could very easily modify them to suit your own décor. The insects are stitched in lustrous space-dyed silks to contrast with the matt finish of the wool.

you will need

Fabric 22 x 24in (55 x 60cm) rectangle of pure linen twill

Appleton crewel wool (yarn)
Light coral 205 – 2 skeins
Dark coral 207 – 2 skeins
Light gold 695 – 2 skeins
Dark gold 696 – 1 skein
Light mauve 714 – 1 skein
Dark mauve 715 – 1 skein
Light green 332 – 3 skeins
Mid green 334 – 3 skeins

Dark green 336 – 2 skeins
Light blue-green 154 – 3 skeins
Dark blue-green 156 – 3 skeins

21st Century Yarns Reflections hand-dyed silk
Fiesta – 1 x 10m skein
Woodland – 1 x 10m skein
Flame – 1 x 10m skein
Kashmir – 1 x 10m skein
Cranberry – 1 x 10m skein
Beech – 1 x 10m skein

Equipment
Size 7 crewel needle
Size 24 tapestry needle
Embroidery frame

Stitches Long and short stitch, stem stitch, split back stitch, fly stitch, open fly stitch, satin stitch, buttonhole stitch, Jacobean couching, chain stitch, straight spider's web stitch and French knots.

Threads Use one strand of crewel wool unless specified otherwise in the instructions. Use one strand of silk for the insects and bulrushes.

Before you begin Prepare your fabric then trace the outline on to it (see pages 102-105). Mount it in your frame. Read the general working advice on page 88.

instructions

the tree

1 Using two strands of mid green outline each leaf in split back stitch. Still using two strands of mid green work a row of long and short stitch around the leaf, taking your stitches over the split back stitch. The split back stitch gives a raised effect and makes it easier to produce a straight edge with the long and short stitch. Using one strand of light green fill the leaf by

working a second row of long and short stitch. Do not leave a gap for the central vein which is worked on top later.

2 For the open fruit use dark coral to work straight spider's web stitch between the parallel lines. Lay plenty of horizontal threads. You will find it easier to change to a fine tapestry needle to weave the whipping thread around the laid bars. You can work up and down and do not worry that the first rows look uneven. You will need to weave more rows in the middle section than at each end – as the bars become full leave them out. Pack the bars tightly so that they begin to stand away from the fabric.

3 Fill the central area of these fruit with light gold long and short stitch. Cover this with dark mauve Jacobean couching held down with dark blue-green. First lay a trellis of long stitches over the light gold in dark mauve. Lay all the stitches in one direction and then lay those in the other direction on top. You will find it easier if you lay the first thread in each direction across the middle of the shape and then fill to each side rather than trying to start with a short stitch across an edge. Couch down each intersection of the threads with a tiny upright cross stitch in dark blue-green.

4 Work the outer sections of the fruit in light coral using long and short stitch. Take care with the direction of your

stitches – they should radiate out of the top of the fruit and turn in again at the bottom.

5 Work light mauve split back stitch around the petals at the top of the fruit and then work a row of long and short stitch over it. Fill the petals with a second row of long and short stitch in dark mauve. Use two strands of dark gold to fill between the petals with tightly packed French knots.

6 Work the sepals immediately below the fruit in the same way as the leaves then add a vein using two strands of dark green stem stitch. Outline the lower sepals with dark green split back stitch and then fill with fly stitch. Use two strands of light blue-green to fill the circle at the base of the fruit with French knots. Use dark blue-green to fill the two lower circles in the same way.

7 For the closed fruit use dark coral to work a row of chain stitch along the lines that divide the centre section. Work close lines inside this in dark and light gold. Taking care with the direction of your stitches as before, fill the centre section with dark coral long and short stitch and the outer sections of the fruit with light coral long and short stitch.

8 Outline the outer two petals at the top of the fruit in dark mauve split back stitch and then fill with fly stitch. Work the central petal in the same way but with light mauve.

9 Work the sepals at the base in dark blue-green satin stitch to the inner line. Then use dark gold to work open fly stitch down the middle of the central sepal and buttonhole stitch along the outer edge of the other two. Finish the edge of these panels in light mauve stem stitch.

10 The tree trunk, branches and leaf veins are all worked in stem stitch using two strands. Use light, mid and dark green and dark gold. Add shape to the trunk by keeping the dark green on the right side and using lighter colours on the left. Use the photograph to help you place each colour. Begin stitching at the base of the trunk and take care where the branches split away from each other. Try to stitch from trunk to branch and then out into a leaf vein all in one go. Do not join on again where the branches split or your tree will look as though the sections were stuck together. Allow the stem stitch to peter out as you reach the leaves so that the veins are thicker at the base of the leaf with only one line at the top.

the landscape

11 Outline the hillocks in split back stitch using two strands of dark blue-green and then work a row of long and short stitch over the top. Complete the hillock on the right with a row of light blue-green long and short stitch using two strands. For the hillock on the left work a row of light blue-green and a row of mid green. For the central one use dark and light blue-green, mid and dark green.

12 Outline the lower leaves of the lily with dark green split back stitch. Fill these leaves with matching fly stitch. Work the two upper leaves in the same way using mid green. Outline all the flower petals in light gold split back stitch and then fill to the vein with satin stitch worked over the split back stitch. Add dark coral stem stitch veins to the three upper petals. For the stamens use dark mauve stem stitch and add three French knots to the end of each one. Work the stem of the lily with two rows of stem stitch using two strands – one of mid green and one of dark gold.

13 Outline the strawberry leaves in split back stitch, using dark green for the lower ones, mid green for the three upper ones and light green for the sepals. Fill the lower leaves with dark green fly stitch, the upper three with mid green satin stitch and the sepals with light green fly stitch. Work the stems and leaf veins in dark green stem stitch. Fill the strawberry with dark coral long and short stitch and then add a scattering of light gold French knots.

14 Work the long leaves of the bulrushes in mid green stem stitch, then add a shorter length of dark green to each leaf to thicken it towards the base. Cover the area of the bulrush heads with tightly packed French knots in beech silk. Work the stems in dark gold stem stitch. Add a few little straight stitches at the base of the French knots to join well and work a stitch at the top to finish each bulrush head.

15 Using two strands of mid green add French knots to the base of the tree trunk, the base of each fruit and the base of the lily. These disguise the joins and make the tree look more natural.

the insects

16 Work the dragonfly's wings in fiesta silk, using long and short stitch for the upper wings and satin stitch for the lower wings. Work the rest of the dragonfly in cranberry silk. For the lower body (abdomen) and head use long and short stitch, for the upper body (thorax) use tightly packed French knots and for the feelers use stem stitch with a single French knot on the end of each one.

17 For the little beetle use woodland silk to fill the outer casing with long and short stitch. For the rest of the beetle use beech silk. Work the lower body in long and short stitch with a line of split back stitch between the sections of the casing. For the head add a cluster of French knots and work the legs with tiny straight stitches. Use stem stitch for the feelers with a French knot at the end of each one.

18 Work the ladybird in the same way as the beetle using flame silk instead of woodland silk and adding French knots for the spots.

19 Now for the butterfly. Use Kashmir silk worked in long and short stitch for the wings. Work the abdomen in long and

short stitch using cranberry silk and fill the thorax with cranberry French knots, adding more in Kashmir to pack the area really tightly. Use beech to work the head in satin stitch and the legs and feelers in stem stitch with a French knot at the end of each one.

20 Finally, work the body of the grasshopper in woodland silk long and short stitch and use fiesta long and short stitch for the head and upper legs. Work the lower legs, front legs and feelers in beech stem stitch. Outline the head in beech stem stitch and add French knots at the end of each feeler. Add one more French knot for an eye.

F I N I S H I N G   O F F

When you have finished the embroidery wash and press it carefully to remove any wrinkles (see page 91). Mount and frame as required. I mounted my piece as a fire screen, but it would work equally well as a picture or made into a cushion.

Leaves and Acorns

*A*ustralian crewel wool is a lovely soft hand-dyed yarn which combines beautifully with couched silk variegated thread for this pair of small projects. I've chosen warm, earthy colours for the curtain tieback which go with my peach coloured fabric, but you can easily change them to suit your decor. The little acorn key fob makes a lovely decorative touch, especially for an antique key. Again you can copy the colours I've used or select your own.

Leafy Curtain Tieback

you will need

Fabric 12 x 30in (30 x 75cm) rectangle of pure linen twill or more if you want long tiebacks for full curtains

Cascade House Australian crewel wool (yarn)
Gold 2180 – 1 skein
Golden brown 2380 – 1 skein
Light green 7510 – 1 skein
Dark green 7250 – 1 skein
Purple 5370 – 1 skein

Mauve 4570 – 1 skein
Rust 3240 – 1 skein

Melange silk
Colour 4140 – 1 skein

Equipment
Size 7 crewel needle
Embroidery hoop or frame

Stitches Long and short stitch, stem stitch, split back stitch, satin stitch, fly stitch, open fly stitch, spider's web stitch, chain stitch, detached chain stitch, bullion knots, Jacobean couching, buttonhole stitch, detached buttonhole stitch, seeding and French knots.

Threads The threads listed are sufficient for one tieback. Use one strand of crewel wool throughout or one strand of silk. You will have enough wool left over to complete the key fob as well if you wish.

Before you begin Prepare your fabric then trace the outline on to it (see page 106). Mount it in your hoop or frame. Read the general working advice on page 88.

instructions

1 Outline the largest leaf in light green split back stitch. Work a row of light green long and short stitch around the edge, taking your stitches over the split back stitch. The split back stitch gives a raised effect and makes it easier to produce a straight edge with the long and short stitch. Finish filling the leaf with dark green long and short stitch.

2 Outline the flourish above the leaf in mauve stem stitch. Outline the small leaves inside it with gold split back stitch and then fill them with gold fly stitch. Work the stem in matching stem stitch. Fill the rest of the shape with rust seeding. Repeat

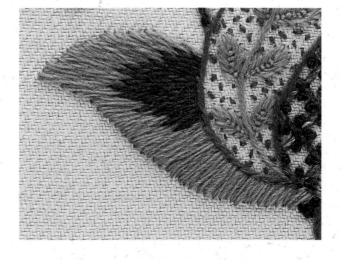

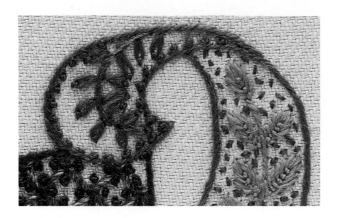

7 Outline all the small leaves in split back stitch in either light or dark green, referring to the photograph for the colours used or selecting your own. Fill them with matching satin stitch.

8 Work a row of rust long and short stitch at the top of the seed heads and then complete with gold. The stitches should radiate out at the top and turn in again at the bottom of each seed head. Fill the tops with tightly packed purple French knots.

9 Work the stems in light and dark green stem stitch, letting your lines run on into the leaf veins so that the leaves join on to the stems naturally. Use the photograph to place the colours. Where the stems join the seed heads work a few short straight stitches at the base.

to work the similar leaf shape below and for and the lower section of the other similar leaf shape. Continue the mauve stem stitch around the top of that shape.

3 Add rust French knots evenly spaced around the inner edge of the top part of the leaf shape shown above. Add a central stem inside it worked in golden brown stem stitch embellished with detached chain stitches.

4 For this curled form first work an outline of mauve chain stitch. Then work two rows of golden brown, then two rows of purple. Work two rows of purple in the centre and then work the 'spokes' in rust stem stitch.

5 For the central leaf start by working a row of rust buttonhole stitch around the outside and finish the edge with detached buttonhole stitch in gold. Fill the centre shape with open fly stitch in light green, then work light green stem stitch between the ends of the buttonhole stitch and the fly stitch. Add a dark green French knot in each gap of the fly stitch.

6 Cover the remaining part of this section with silk Jacobean couching held down with purple. First lay a trellis of long stitches in silk. Lay all the stitches in one direction and then lay those in the other direction on top. It is easier to lay the first thread in each direction across the middle of the shape and then fill to each side. Couch down each intersection of the threads with a tiny upright cross stitch in purple. Decorate each intersection with four dark green French knots.

10 Work rust satin stitch around the outer section of these forms, then fill the centres with gold bullion knots. Start the bullion knots at the tip of each shape and then fill well, overlapping the knots and allowing them to spill over on to the rust. Work evenly spaced purple French knots around the edge.

11 Fill the circles at the base with purple spider's web stitch. Pack the spokes of the web tightly to raise the shape off the fabric.

F I N I S H I N G   O F F

When you have finished the embroidery wash and press it carefully to remove any wrinkles (see page 91). To assemble the tieback see the instructions on page 114.

Acorn Key Fob

Fabric 4in (10cm) square of pure linen twill

Cascade House Australian crewel wool (yarn)
Gold 2180 – 1 skein
Golden brown 2380 – 1 skein
Light green 7510 – 1 skein
Dark green 7250 – 1 skein

Purple 5370 – 1 skein
Rust 3240 – 1 skein

Melange silk
Colour 4140 – 1 skein

Equipment
Size 7 crewel needle
Embroidery hoop or frame

Stitches Long and short stitch, stem stitch, split back stitch, satin stitch, Jacobean couching and French knots.

Threads Use one strand of crewel wool throughout or one strand of silk.

Before you begin Prepare your fabric then trace the outline on to it (see below). Mount it in your hoop or frame. Read the general working advice on page 88.

instructions

1 Start by outlining the leaf with dark green split back stitch. Work a row of dark green long and short stitch around the edge, taking your stitches over the split back stitch. The split back stitch gives a raised effect and makes it easier to produce a straight edge with the long and short stitch. Fill the rest of the leaf with a row of light green long and short stitch.

2 Work the stem and vein in dark green stem stitch with two rows for the vein and three rows for the stem.

3 Work the tops of the acorns in gold satin stitch and then cover the acorn cups in golden brown French knots. Add rust French knots to fill the gaps, packing them in tightly.

4 Fill the square with silk Jacobean couching held down with purple. First lay a trellis of long stitches from the points marked on the drawing. Lay all the stitches in one direction and then lay those in the other direction on top. Couch down each intersection of the threads with a tiny upright cross stitch in purple. Couch a straight thread along each side of the square and then edge it with dark green stem stitch. Work a dark green French knot in the centre of each little diamond and add one at each intersection and corner around the edge.

FINISHING OFF

When you have finished the embroidery wash and press it carefully to remove any wrinkles (see page 91). To assemble the embroidery as a key fob follow the instructions on page 114.

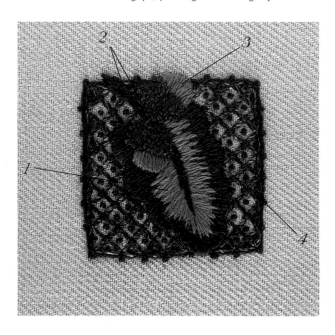

Jacobean Tieback

*T*his elegant design was inspired by many examples from early Jacobean embroidery when we had blue dye from woad. The colour was not constant then and there was always colour variation that gave depth to the design. I used three shades of blue to recreate this effect but you can use three shades of any colour to tie in with your décor. Of course, you don't have to use this design on a tieback – frame it as a picture or make it into a cushion, for example.

Jacobean Tieback

you will need

Fabric 12 x 30in (30 x 75cm) rectangle of pure linen twill or more if you want long tiebacks for full curtains

Cascade House Australian crewel wool (yarn)
Mid blue 9540 – 1 skein

Light blue 9480 – 2 skeins
Dark blue 9560 – 2 skeins

Equipment
Size 7 crewel needle
Embroidery hoop or frame

Stitches Long and short stitch, stem stitch, split back stitch, fly stitch, open fly stitch, pearl stitch, chain stitch, detached chain stitch, double cross stitch, fern stitch, Jacobean couching, seeding and French knots.

Threads Use one strand of crewel wool throughout or one strand of silk.

Before you begin Prepare your fabric then trace the outline on to it (see page 107). Mount it in your hoop or frame.

instructions

1 Work a row of light blue split back stitch on the top edges of the darkest petals. Work a row of light blue long and short stitch along these edges, taking your stitches over the split back stitch. The split back stitch gives a raised effect and makes it easier to produce a straight edge with the long and short stitch. Work a second row on the two larger petals. Fill all three with long and short stitch, working through mid blue to dark blue at the base.

2 Outline this petal with dark blue stem stitch and then fill the centre with mid blue fern stitch. The pattern provides the skeleton lines of the fern stitch; add the little leaf shapes as you go, using the photograph as a guide.

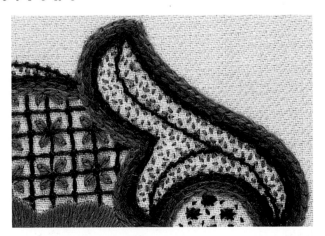

3 Outline these petals with light blue chain stitch and add close lines inside in mid and dark blue. Work the veins in dark blue pearl stitch and fill with light blue seeding.

83

4 Fill the central petal with dark blue Jacobean couching. First lay a trellis of long stitches. Lay all the stitches in one direction and then lay those in the other direction on top. You will find it easier if you lay the first thread in each direction across the middle of the shape and then fill to each side rather than trying to start with a short stitch across an edge. Couch down each intersection of the threads with a tiny upright cross stitch also in dark blue. Work four detached chain stitches in light blue at every other intersection.

5 Using dark blue fill the final petal with randomly spaced double cross stitches and then fill in with dark blue seeding.

6 Outline these small leaves in dark blue split back stitch and then fill with fly stitch.

7 Outline the large leaf at the base of the stem with light blue split back stitch and then fill with light blue long and short stitch, shading through mid to dark blue at the centre. Work the vein in dark blue stem stitch.

8 Work the main stem with four rows of dark blue stem stitch, two rows of mid blue and a final row of dark blue. Add the stem for the leaves near the base with a line of dark blue stem stitch, working so that the leaves seem to grown from it.

9 Outline the remaining leaves in pearl stitch, using dark blue for the two outer ones and mid blue for the centre one. Fill each leaf with mid blue open fly stitch and then add a mid blue French knot in each axle. Work the stems for these leaves in dark and mid blue stem stitch, using the photograph as a guide.

F I N I S H I N G   O F F

When you have finished the embroidery wash and press it carefully to remove any wrinkles (see page 91). To assemble the tieback refer to the instructions on page 114.

chapter six

Working the Projects

*E*ach project in this book comes with details of which stitches to use and which wools (yarns) to buy, as well as step-by-step instructions. However, if your are a beginner you may want a bit more help which is what this section is for. You may also find it worth refreshing your memory by reading this section even if you are an experienced embroiderer – a simple tip here may transform your working methods and stitching results.

Equipment and Techniques

'A good workman never blames his tools', or so the saying goes, but I find that when it comes to embroidery the tools and equipment really do make a difference. There is nothing worse than working with unsuitable fabrics or threads or using the wrong needle – you simply won't be able to get satisfactory results. This brief guide outlines your choices of materials and equipment and explains how to make the most out of them.

Fabrics

Pure linen twill This is the traditional fabric used for crewel embroidery. It is quite a thick, dense fabric and the weave is very close so the threads of the fabric close up around the stitches. It is only available in one colour, a natural golden shade, which provides a beautiful, flattering background for most colours. It is also the easiest fabric to work on and if you are new to crewel embroidery I suggest that you begin on this.

Silk dupion I have used this for several of the designs in this book. I like the slubbed texture, the natural sheen and the huge range of colours available, and I'm quite sure that in Jacobean times embroiderers would have jumped at the chance of using it if it had been available.

Other choices In general I think you should stick to natural fibres rather than synthetic ones for your embroidery, but if you want to try something new be guided by your local embroidery shop and ask for a fabric suitable for surface embroidery. Make sure your fabric has a close weave so that the threads will not separate as you stitch. If you are in doubt, try stitching a small sample before you go to the trouble of tracing out a design only to find that you don't like the fabric.

Threads

Crewel wool The dictionary defines crewel as 'a loosely twisted worsted yarn used in embroidery', so traditionally crewelwork has always been done using crewel wool (yarn). There are several types on the market. I have mainly chosen Appleton's crewel wool because of its availability and superb colour range. If you particularly want to use another range, refer to the colours in the line drawings to help you. Note that the finer the yarn the easier it is to give your stitching a smooth look so don't be tempted to finish more quickly by buying a thicker yarn.

Other options Wool yarn was used on linen traditionally because that was what we could produce in our climate. I make no excuses to traditionalists when I use stranded cottons, silks and metallic thread as well as wool, combining them to good effect. If you prefer alternative threads then use them but do note that they are not as forgiving as wool, so if you are a beginner wool may be the best first choice.

Embroidery frames and hoops

It is vital to keep your fabric taut as some of the stitches used are quite long and it is easy to bunch up the fabric if it is not held tight. For this reason always mount your fabric in a frame or hoop.

Hoops These are ideal for fairly small designs. When mounting the fabric always make sure that the entire design is well within the stitching area – don't try to fit a hoop over worked areas as it may damage your stitches and will not secure the fabric evenly over the thickness of the embroidery. If this isn't possible change to a larger hoop or move up to a frame.

Rectangular frames You'll need a frame to work large designs. There is a good selection to choose from including rotating and upholstered frames. Rotating frames are quite inexpensive

and come in many sizes. The fabric is stitched to webbing along the width of the frame and laced to the side bars. Excess fabric is taken up by rollers at the top and bottom. These can be used as they are or mounted on legs to stand on the floor. Experiment with different types to find what suits you. The best one is the one you are most comfortable with and which enables you to work for as long as you like without back, shoulder or neck discomfort. Another choice is an upholstered frame which is what I like best. These enable you to work on an embroidery of any size. Just pin the area to be worked on the frame and move it as work progresses. The padding is comfortable to rest on and the frame makes an attractive feature in your living room.

Line drawings

The line drawings in this book are in colour to give you an idea of which yarn to use where. There are also accompanying photographs of the finished piece which provide a good reference for shading. Don't be frightened by the absence of any lines to follow; once you start you will be surprised how easy it is and how creative you can be.

Tracing an Outline on to Fabric

you will need

Black felt-tip pen
Water-soluble pen
Sheet of tracing paper
Masking tape

instructions

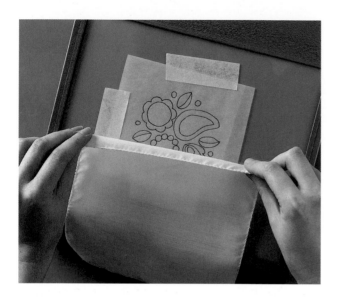

1 Trace the outline of your chosen design on to tracing paper with a black felt-tip pen. Tape the tracing to an artist's light box and tape the fabric on top so you can trace the outlines on to the fabric. Alternatively, use daylight as your source of light by taping the tracing to a window pane and then taping the fabric over it. (Some photographic slide viewers work well for this or you can also use a blank but illuminated computer screen.)

2 Go over the lines of the design with your water-soluble pen. This leaves a strong blue line on the fabric that is easy to see but as soon as it comes into contact with water it completely disappears. Be careful because if you put your partly finished work aside the moisture in the air gradually works on the pen lines too, and eventually your lovely drawing will vanish. If the water-soluble pen lines don't show on the fabric because of its colour, use a permanent pen. This is what I did for the parrot waistcoat on page 56. Make sure

your pen is permanent and waterproof and cover the design lines with your stitching as you work.

General working advice

Split back stitch This is used to outline areas which will be filled with long and short stitch. It is better than back stitch for making smooth curves and for producing a line of even thickness. The split back stitch acts as a padding and will be completely covered when the embroidery is finished. It also makes it easier to line up the stitches of the long and short stitch which follows.

Long and short stitch This stitch enables you to shade and blend colours. To begin, come up through the fabric on the outside and go down towards the centre. Work subsequent rows from the centre outwards. A long stitch should alternate with a short one, but don't be too rigid about this. Imagine you are painting and that the stitches are random brush strokes on the canvas. When working this stitch always split the threads of each previous row of stitching to ensure a good blending of colour and to give a smooth finish. You stitches should be longer than feels necessary because they will be shortened by the following row of stitches. The idea that good stitches are small ones does not apply to long and short stitch. In order for threads to lie smoothly the stitches need to be long enough to lie flat. (See Working with Crewel Wool below.)

Breaking yarns If your yarn seems to get thin and break easily it is probably because you are allowing the plies to untwist as you stitch. Drop the needle every so often to let the yarn twist up naturally. Alternatively, give the needle a tiny turn as you make each stitch, as I do. Once you have done this for a while it becomes second nature and you do it automatically.

Stitch direction As you work be aware of the direction of each stitch and make sure the stitches of each row follow the same direction as those in the previous one. As a general rule, try to stitch the design in the direction of growth or follow the way fur or feathers lie. You'll obtain a much better result. For a flower or leaf stitches should seem to radiate out from the centre. You will have to overlap some towards the centre to achieve this.

Leaf veins These should be worked on top of the stitched leaf. Since you will have covered the stitching line with embroidery use the photograph or line drawing as a guide.

Filling gaps Fill any gaps between leaves or flowers and stems with a few French knots. This is a useful way of making two sets of stitching join together so the leaf looks as though it grew from the stem and was not just stuck on.

S T A R T I N G   &   F I N I S H I N G

Start your stitching using a knot on the top and working towards it so that the long stitch on the back is covered with stitches. When you near the knot cut it away. Alternatively, do as I do and leave the knot on the top of the fabric about 4in (10cm) from where you intend to start stitching. Once there is enough stitching on the fabric you can cut off the knot and thread the short length into the needle. Work this into the back of the stitching. To begin and finish off after this simply run the yarn through the back of the stitching that is already completed.

Working with Crewel Wool

This example shows how I work my embroidery. You don't have to work in exactly the same way but my experience has shown that this is the easiest and most effective method for me.

1 Use split back stitch to outline areas which will be filled with long and short stitch. This enables you to get a neat edge and pads the long and short stitch which is worked on top.

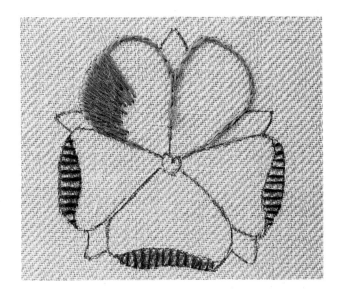

2 Begin the long and short stitch by bringing your needle up at the outer edge and going down towards the centre of the flower or leaf. The stitches should be closer together towards the centre and you will need to overlap them to achieve this. Your short stitches will seem to disappear between the longer ones. Notice how long the stitches are – they will be shortened by the next row. I have also started the straight spider's stitch at this stage. Make quite closely spaced bars, as shown.

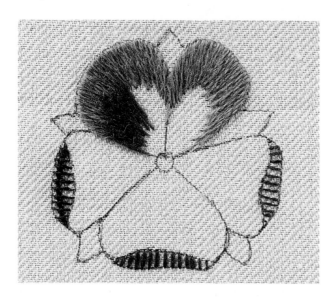

3   I work the second and subsequent rows of long and short stitch from the centre of the flower or leaf outwards. Working in this way enables you to see what you are doing. Each stitch should split the threads of the previous row of stitching. It is much easier to split the threads from above rather than trying to spear them unseen from below. Also, if your thread raises any fluff this will be taken to the back of your work rather than being left on the front. For the straight spider's stitch I begin to weave the bars at this stage (see the photograph above). You can work up and down and don't worry that it doesn't look very tidy to start with. Pull the weaving thread quite tightly.

4   The pale mauve long and short stitch shown above right is coming from a small area towards the flower centre and spreading out towards the edge of the petals. Notice how every stitch seems to radiate out of the centre of the flower. Now the weaving on the laid bars of the straight spider's stitch is packed very tightly so the whole area seems to lift off the surface. As the shorter bars at the ends get full just leave them out and carry on weaving on the longer ones.

Working with Stranded Cotton or Silk

This technique is exactly the same as when working with wool. Take care that your long and short stitches are very close and parallel because cottons and silks are considerably less forgiving than wool .

1   Use split back stitch to outline areas which will be filled with long and short stitch. This enables you to produce a very neat edge and pads the long and short stitch which is worked over the top.

above rather than trying to spear them unseen from below. Also, if your thread raises any fluff this will be taken to the back of your work out of sight rather than being left on the front.

2 Begin the long and short stitch by bringing your needle up at the outer edge and going down towards the centre of the flower or leaf. The stitches should be closer together towards the centre where the petal or leaf gets narrower and you will need to overlap them to achieve this. Your short stitches will seem to disappear between the longer ones. Notice how long the stitches are – they will be shortened by the next row.

4 Work the stems in stem stitch, beginning at the bottom of the stem and work out to the tip of the tendril. Then begin again at the bottom and work out into the leaf. Wherever stems branch try to begin your stem stitch as near to the bottom of the plant as possible and carry on out into the branches or leaf. This way the plant will look as if it grew rather than as if it was stuck together.

Finishing the embroidery

Washing It is advisable to wash crewelwork once you have completed the stitching. If you have used the tracing method to transfer the design to the fabric this will wash away the pen lines. Also washing with a gentle, bleach-free soap will freshen the piece and usually makes the stitch tension more even. Rinse the embroidery well in hand-hot water and lay it on a towel. Roll up the towel with the embroidery in it to remove excess moisture and then unroll and allow the embroidery to dry naturally.

Pressing If your piece is fairly small, ironing should be sufficient to remove creases and puckers caused by the stitching, but if your work is very puckered or quite large you may need to stretch it (see below). Heat the iron to a hot setting,

3 I work the second and subsequent rows of long and short stitch from the centre outwards which enables me to see what I am doing. Each stitch should split the threads of the previous row of stitching, as shown. It is much easier to split threads from

cover the ironing board with two layers of towelling and place the embroidery face-down on top. Press firmly using plenty of steam. If you don't have a steam iron, cover the back of the work with a damp cloth and press through the cloth. Never press crewelwork from the right side. Leave the embroidery to cool and dry before framing or making up.

Stretching If you have completed a large piece of crewelwork or have tried ironing and are not satisfied you will need to stretch your embroidery. This will remove puckers within the embroidered area that are difficult to iron out. If in doubt about which method to use choose this one. Although it takes longer it always works.

Stretching a Finished Piece

you will need

Large, flat clean board (chipboard is ideal)
Plenty of ordinary 1in (2.5cm) nails and hammer
Dressmakers' squared paper
Garden plant spray filled with clean water
Masking tape

instructions

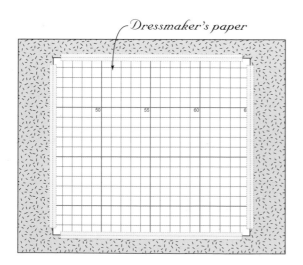

Dressmaker's paper

1 Cover the board with squared paper and secure with masking tape around the edges.

2 Place the embroidery right-side up on top of the squared paper. Your embroidery should be completely dry; linen becomes slightly stretchy when wet and it is possible to over stretch it if it is damp.

3 Begin nailing in one corner near the edge of the fabric, using the lines on the paper to keep the fabric straight and nailing into every second intersection of a line on the paper, as shown. It is important that the nails are no more than ¾in (2cm) apart.

4 Finish the first side and then return to the corner and repeat exactly the same process on the adjacent edge (at right angles), again keeping the fabric grain straight.

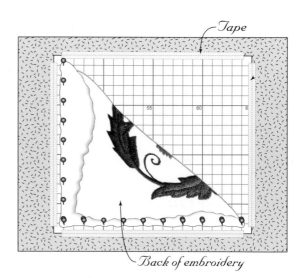

Tape

Back of embroidery

5 Fold down embroidery diagonally and use the squares on the paper to establish where the last corner should be.

6   Replace the embroidery, nail the last corner in place and then finish nailing the remaining two sides.

7   Dampen the whole area using a spray (such as a plant spray) filled with ordinary tap water. Make sure that both the embroidered area and the unworked area are uniformly wet to ensure an even stretch.

8   Don't worry if the fabric seems to stretch and go loose on the nails; it will tighten as it dries and remove all the creases. Allow to dry completely and then remove the nails.

Design Ideas

The free nature of crewel embroidery makes it the perfect technique for adaptation. Gone are the charts or painted lines which give you no choices. Instead you follow simple line drawings. You decide where to put your needle and even if you work the same design twice you'll find it looks different. Even so, you may want to take your creativity further and come up with your own designs and colourways. Here are some hints and tips to get you started.

If you are new to this type of stitching then it is a good idea to follow one of the designs from this book exactly, using all the specified colours. Later, when you have mastered the stitches and learned to let go a little, why not choose your own colours and stitches and even come up with your own designs.

If you need some inspiration for your own designs, just look around you. We are surrounded by a wealth of design sources – wallpaper, curtain fabrics, books, greetings cards and so on. This means that even if you can't draw confidently you can still copy or adapt images already available. All you need is a very simple outline drawing which can be obtained by tracing – the size can then be altered on a photocopier if necessary. Look out for free-flowing and curved shapes rather than linear and angled ones which don't work as well in crewelwork.

When taking a design from textured fabric you may find it easiest to photocopy the fabric either in colour or black and white so that you have the shapes on paper. At this stage you are just looking at the overall shape and not at the detail,

so make a very simple outline tracing. By using this method you can make embroidered cushion fronts to go with your furnishing fabrics or curtain tiebacks to go with your curtains and so on.

Take care with the size of your chosen design. Look at it carefully and study the areas to be covered. Are they so big that you will need to work too much of the same thing and make an uninteresting composition or are they so small that you can't to get any recognisable stitches in? In either case you can get round the problem by reducing or enlarging the design on a photocopier.

I think that a lot of effort put in at this stage pays dividends later. There is nothing worse than wishing a piece was slightly different once you have finished. If I have doubts then the design probably needs changing. For me I find it helps if I leave a drawing, or even a partly worked piece, propped up where it will 'surprise' me later as I walk past. Often this enables me to see more clearly what is causing the doubt because I am able to see it afresh and with 'new' eyes.

My hope is that this book will be just the start for you and that once you have tried some of my designs you will begin to realise that this type of embroidery is much easier than it looks. There is nothing to compare with the satisfaction of working a piece that is unique and yours.

Compiling several designs into one

It is very easy to assemble a large design from several smaller ones which is what I did for the bell pull on page 24. In that case the curving shapes of the individual motifs made it easier to combine them. I traced all the designs and then laid the tracings together and just rearranged them until I was happy with the result. I also added a fifth design – the tulip – because odd numbers always look better than even numbers. (Nature knows this as well – count the numbers of petals on flowers which will nearly always be odd.) Finally, I rearranged the stems through the design so that they ran smoothly from one to the next but retained the curves. You can do the same using a selection of several motifs which you like.

In the case of the bell pull I also reversed the design – the individual fruits and flowers are actually mirror images of the originals. This is also a useful technique and it's very easy to do. Just flip the tracing over. You could use this method to stitch a pair of designs to sit either side of you fireplace, for instance, or to make tiebacks for each side of the window.

Selecting the colours

When choosing the threads for a project you have designed yourself you will find that most ranges are displayed so that the shades of one colour are next to each other. Take heed of this and choose two or three shades of a colour. Hold all the colours that you want to use together and look at them in a

bundle; look at the ends of the skeins away from the labels so that you only see the colours. If at this stage there is one that seems to 'shout' it will do so when stitched. Do you want it to? If not put it back and choose a softer shade. Again take plenty of time over this.

You will also find that some colours seem to change as you stitch with them and as they interact with your other colours – if you do not like the effect change it because it will always nag at you later and you will wish that you had.

I would also advise that you beware of thrift with threads. Most of us are conditioned to make do with what we have or buy items which are on special offer. It is a false economy to use the colours that you have or can buy cheaply rather than the ones you would like – the result will always seem second rate. Rather than be in any doubt buy more colours to add to your collection. I take as much pleasure from a selection of threads as from the finished pieces. After all, who knows what they will inspire later.

Peony Jacket – page 10

Fruits and Flowers
Bell Pull — page 24

Lion and Unicorn Workbox – page 40

Parrot Waistcoat – page 56

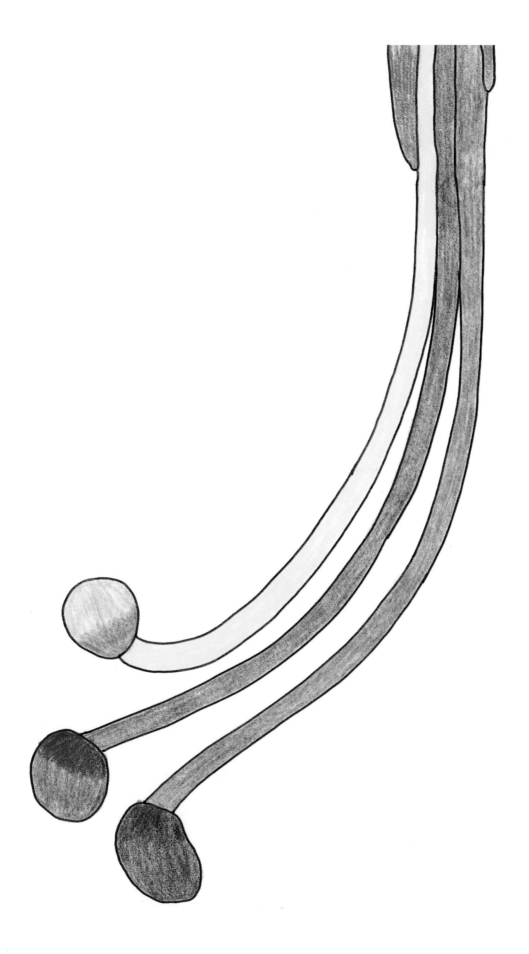

Tree of Life Fire Screen – page 72

Tree of Life Fire Screen (continued)

Leafy Tieback –
page 79

Jacobean Tieback –
page 83

chapter seven

Making up the Projects

I believe that an embroidery is really only about half done once the stitching is finished. The rest of the job lies in the presentation. I take enormous trouble to find the right fabrics or frames and then think carefully about how I can embellish my work to show it off to best advantage. Don't be content to stick your work in a frame and hang it on the wall. Use fabrics and braids for trimming that bring out its colours and provide a link with your furnishings. I am quite shameless about buying fabrics and trimmings and have cupboards full, but I have to say that they all get used eventually. So make your purchase, enjoy owning a beautiful piece of fabric and buy a bigger cupboard if need be.

Mounting Ready for Framing

you will need

Frame
Mount board (polyboard is ideal)
Double-sided tape
Polyester wadding (optional)
Dressmakers' pins
Craft knife

instructions

1 Select your frame. Either buy one ready-made or have one custom-made. Obviously a ready-made frame is cheaper but a custom-made one will probably look better. Select your board for mounting and cut it to fit the frame. I like to use polyboard (lightweight foam core) which is made from two sheets of card with a thin layer of polystyrene in-between. The polystyrene layer is easy to pin into and because the board is light it is also very easy to cut to size.

2 All the framed projects in this book have been padded. This is because the back of crewelwork tends to be quite thick and padding absorbs some of this thickness, ensuring that the front looks smooth. The raised surface also presents well in a frame. To pad the board simply cut polyester wadding the same size and attach it to the board with double-sided tape. If you are using a mount only pad the area that will appear in the aperture. Use the mount to help you position it on the backing board.

3 Lay the embroidery over the mount board and centre it by measuring. Check the effect by eye because sometimes a design looks unbalanced even if the measurements are correct. Adjust as necessary so it looks right. Use dressmakers' pins to pin through the embroidery into the edge of the board. Place one in the centre of each edge and then work out to the corners, making sure that the fabric grain is straight. Time and care taken at this stage is well spent, so make sure you are entirely happy with the effect before continuing.

4 Turn the board over and trim the excess fabric, leaving about 1½in (4cm) all round. Secure tightly with double-sided tape or by lacing across the back with strong thread. Remove the pins.

5 If you wish to mount your work under glass and pad it too you will need to put spacers in the frame between the embroidery and the glass to prevent the padding pushing the embroidery against the underside of the glass. Your framer should be able to advise you on this.

Making a Covered Mount

you will need

Picture mount
Polyester wadding
Lightweight fabric larger than the mount in each direction
Double-sided tape
Dressmakers' pins
Clear multi-purpose glue (optional)

instructions

1 Select your mount. It may come with the frame or you can ask a framer to cut one for you. Alternatively, cut your

own using a craft knife if you have a steady hand. Cover the mount with polyester wadding cut to fit, attaching it with double-sided tape.

2 Lay your fabric over the padded mount and pin the sides in the same way as you mounted the embroidery (see step 3, above left). Ignore the aperture in the middle of the mount for the moment. Make sure the fabric grain is straight. Secure the fabric on the back with double-sided tape, then remove the pins.

3 Cut out the central area, leaving a margin of ¾in (2cm) around the aperture. If the aperture is round or oval snip into this margin at intervals for ease, but do not clip right up to the mount. For square or rectangular apertures snip to the corners, but again don't go right up to the mount. Turn in the edges and secure on the back with double-sided tape.

4 If you wish, decorate the edge of the aperture with a twisted cord. You can make your own cord from thread which matches the fabric or picks up colours from the embroidery (see below). Fold the cord in half to find the mid point and pin this to the top centre of the aperture. Use clear multi-purpose glue in tiny blobs to attach the cord, starting at the top to stick it round one side and then returning to the top to start sticking it round the other side. Tuck the two ends together and take them to the back at the centre of the bottom edge. Glue them down as well. Alternatively, stitch the cord on with fine sewing thread.

Making a Twisted Cord (Monk's Cord)

you will need
Thread in any colour(s) or a combination of threads

instructions

1 Decide on the length and thickness of the cord. You'll need enough strands to make a bunch of half the desired thickness. Cut them three times the finished length.

2 Tie a knot at both ends of the bunch of threads. Secure one end to a door knob or hook or ask a friend to hold it. Twist the other end until the thread begins to double back on itself when you can let the tension off slightly.

3 Fold the strands in half, letting go of the centre point carefully and holding the two ends together. The cord will twist and you should tie the loose ends together without letting them go. (If you need to cut the cord make sure that the end is knotted or the cord will unravel.)

Alternative cords

For a thick cord start with a longer length and twist and fold it twice. If you want to use twists of different colours, make two cords of half thickness and join them together so the twist runs in the same direction along the length. Twist again and fold as before.

Making Tassels

y o u   w i l l   n e e d

Card and scissors
Thread in your chosen colours

i n s t r u c t i o n s

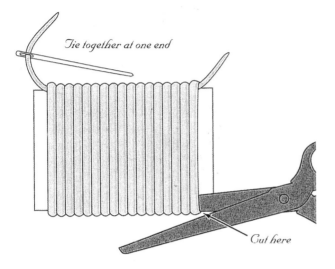

Tie together at one end

Cut here

1   Cut a piece of card longer than the required length of the tassel and whatever width you find easy to hold. Starting with the thread end at the bottom of the card, wind the thread around the card until you build up the required thickness. Pass a separate thread under the thread on the card and tie the ends together at the top. Do not cut off the ends of this thread. Cut the thread at the bottom of the card in line with the card edge.

Wind around all threads to make top

2   Take another length of thread and wind it around the bunch near the top to shape the 'knot'. Tie off securely and trim the ends. Trim the tassel to the required length. Use the top tie to secure the tassel – to a scissors keeper, for example.

Assembling the Bell Pull

y o u   w i l l   n e e d

8in (20cm) bell pull ends or adjustable-length ones, as shown
10 x 27½in (25 x 70cm) rectangle of curtain lining or fine cotton
8 x 24in (20 x 62cm) rectangle of heavy-weight interfacing
Sewing thread
Dressmakers' pins
Pencil and ruler

i n s t r u c t i o n s

1   If you are using fixed-length ends measure the exact length and take off a bit to allow ease for the thickness of your stitching. Cut the interfacing to size, first drawing pencil lines with a ruler to make sure it is perfectly straight. Cut it out carefully. If you are using adjustable-length ends, follow the manufacturer's instructions for cutting.

2   Place the embroidery face down and lay the interfacing over it so the design is in the centre. Trim the edges of the fabric to allow a 1in (2.5cm) margin all round. Turn these edges over and pin down the long side edges. Catch down these edges with herringbone stitch, taking care to stitch only into the thickness of the interfacing and not into the embroidered side of the bell pull.

3 Turn over the top and bottom ends, enclosing the bell pull ends. Pin and then stitch as before.

4 Lay the lining over the back and trim to leave a margin of about ½in (1.2cm) all round. Turn the edges in so that the lining is just slightly smaller than the bell pull. This ensures that the lining won't show on the right side. Slip stitch the edge of the lining to the turnings of the bell pull.

5 If you wish add a tassel detail. I made twisted cords from the mixed yarns left over from stitching the top and bottom of the bell pull and then made a big fat tassel for the bottom.

Assembling the Pineapple and Pomegranate Cushions

you will need

20in (50cm) square of furnishing fabric or velvet
Cushion pad 1-2in (2.5-5cm) larger than the finished cover
Braid or trimmings to go round all four sides

instructions

1 Measure the embroidery and decide on the size of the finished cushion. Subtract the size of the embroidery from the finished measurement and divide by two to find the width of the border. Add 1¼in (3cm) for seam allowances. Cut four border pieces this width by the finished width of the cushion plus 1¼in (3cm). Then cut a square back piece the finished size of the cushion plus 1¼in (3cm) in each dimension. Finally, cut the embroidery to the required size, adding 1¼in (3cm) to each dimension.

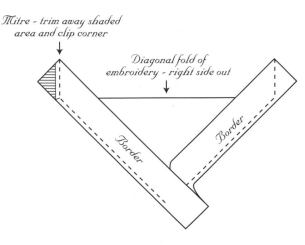

Mitre - trim away shaded area and clip corner

Diagonal fold of embroidery - right side out

Border

Border

2 Find the midpoint of each edge of the embroidery by folding in half and mark with a pin. Fold each border panel in

half to find the centre and mark it with a pin. Matching the pins, pin a border piece to each side of the embroidery. Leave the ends free. With the embroidery uppermost, machine stitch the borders in place, stopping your stitching ⅝in (1.5cm) from each end. Your stitching lines should meet at the corners. Make sure you don't catch the free ends of the border pieces in your stitching.

3   Fold the embroidery in half diagonally with wrong sides together. Mitre each corner of the border by stitching a line from the corners of the embroidery to the diagonally opposite corner of the border, as shown left. Trim off the excess fabric from the borders and clip the corners.

4   Trim the cushion if required. I used braid and a tassel that I top-stitched around the embroidery for the pineapple cushion, while for the pomegranate I inserted a fringe into the edge of the cushion. If you are using an inserted trimming, tack it to the front piece now.

5   Pin the front to the back with right sides facing and stitch around three sides. Turn right sides out and insert the cushion pad. I used a larger cushion pad to give a well-filled look. Slipstitch the remaining side closed. If you are using an applied trimming, stitch it to the edge of the cushion now.

Making the Dragonfly Needlebook

you will need

4¾ x 8¾in (12 x 22cm) rectangle of polyester wadding
Two pieces of felt for the pages 3 x 6in (8 x 16cm)
Twisted cord in dark green and dark purple silks left over from the embroidery 27½in (70cm) long (see page 110)
Pinking shears (optional)

instructions

1   Press the embroidery and trim to make a 4¾ x 8¾in (12 x 22cm) rectangle, centring the design neatly. You may find it easier if you make a paper pattern of the correct dimensions first.

2   Lay out the wadding and then lay the embroidery face up on top. Cover with the fabric. Pin and then stitch around the edge, following the grain of the fabric and leaving an opening in the bottom for turning. Trim the seams, clip the corners and trim the wadding seam allowance right up to the seam to reduce bulk. Turn right sides out.

3   Slip stitch the opening closed, leaving a small gap to tuck in the ends of your cord trim. Tuck one end of the cord into this gap and then catch it carefully all around the edges of the needlebook. Trim to length and then tuck the other end into the gap too.

4   If you have any pinking shears use them to trim the edges of the felt pages. Fold the pages in half to find the centre line and stitch securely to the spine of the book. This stitching should go through the lining only and not into the embroidery.

Making the Bee Scissors Keeper and Acorn Fob

you will need

Backing fabric
Polyester wadding

instructions

1   Press the embroidery and trim to make a 2¾in (7cm) square, centring the design.

2   Cut a piece of backing fabric to match and place right sides together. Pin and then stitch all round, following the grain of the fabric and leaving an opening in one side for turning. Trim the seams, clip the corners and turn right sides out. Stuff the design with polyester wadding and slipstitch the opening closed.

3   Make a 28in (70cm) long twisted cord from your left-over threads (see page 110). Fold the cord in half and tie a knot to attach to the top corner. Slip stitch the knot to the corner and then stitch the loose ends of the cord around the sides. Tie another knot at the bottom corner and then trim the ends. Tease out the threads to make the tassel.

Making the Tiebacks

you will need

20in (50cm) rectangle of lightweight furnishing fabric for backing a pair of tiebacks
Interlining (pelmet interlining is ideal)
4 brass curtain rings (2 for each tieback)
Satin bias binding or bias-cut strips of fabric

instructions

1   Loop a tape measure around the hanging curtain to see how long to make each tieback. If you are not sure cut a trial piece in calico to check the fit. Make a paper pattern by tracing the curve from the edge of the embroidery design and add as much length to the end as you need to accommodate your curtain.

2   Cut the embroidered top, a piece of interlining and a piece of furnishing fabric from your pattern. There is no need to add seam allowances.

3 Lay the embroidery out face down, then place the inter-lining on top and then the backing. Tack all three layers together. Begin at the centre bottom of the tieback to pin the binding on, right sides together, all round the edge. Make a neat join where the ends of the binding meet and then stitch the binding on all round.

4 Trim the edges of the fabric layers and then turn the binding over to the back. Turn in the raw edge of the binding and slipstitch it to the fabric backing.

5 Attach a brass ring to each end of the tieback. If you don't want the rings to show stitch them just inside the edge.

chapter eight

Stitch Library

*H*ere is a guide to working all the stitches required for the projects in this book. They are placed in the order you are most likely to use them when following the step-by-step instructions. You'll find that some of them, such as split back stitch and long and short stitch, are used for every project while other stitches, such as fern stitch and pearl stitch, are used less frequently.

split back stitch

This is similar to ordinary back stitch, except that the needle is inserted into the previous stitch. Bring the needle up at the start of the stitching line (1). Insert it a little way along the line (2), bringing it up one stitch length further along (3).

To work the next and subsequent stitches insert the needle where the previous stitch ended (2), splitting the thread with your needle, then bring it up two stitch lengths further along (4). You'll find that you can produce very smooth curves by making each stitch curve a little as you split it.

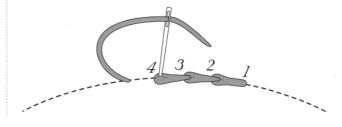

long and short stitch

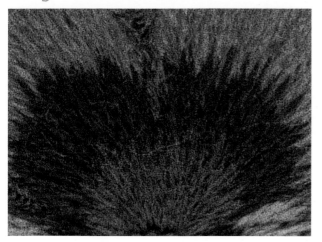

Work as shown. Only the first row has long and short stitches; the subsequent rows are all long. Begin at the outside edge (1) and then stitch subsequent rows into the stitches already worked, splitting the threads to blend the stitches and colours (2). Do not be afraid to make the stitches longer than you feel you should as they will be shortened by the next row of stitching. Do not try to follow the diagrams too rigidly – use them as a guide only because you will have to adapt to the shape that you are filling.

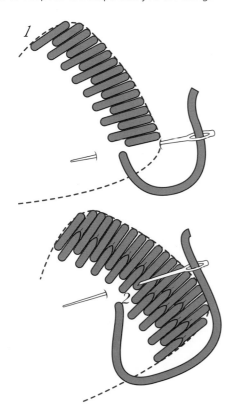

stem stitch

Bring the needle up at the start of the stitching line (1). Take it back down one stitch length along (2) and bring it up halfway along the stitch and slightly to one side (3). Repeat to sew the whole line of overlapping back stitches. Hold the thread down with your finger each time you make a stitch to keep it out of the way and also to maintain an even tension. Try to make your stitches equal in length all along the line unless you are working round a curve in which case it helps to shorten the stitches a little.

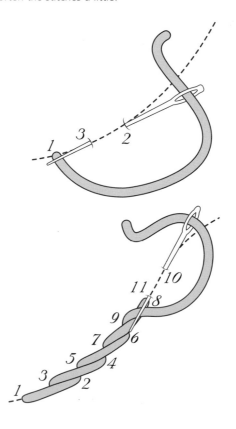

chain stitch

Bring the needle up through the fabric (1). Insert it in the same hole (2) forming a loop of thread as you do so, and bring the needle up in the loop (3), as shown. Pull the thread gently to make the first loop of the chain. Repeat to work the whole chain. Hold the thread as you make each stitch and do not pull the thread too tightly so that the loops remain rounded. To finish the chain catch down the last loop with a small stitch.

detached chain stitch (lazy daisy)

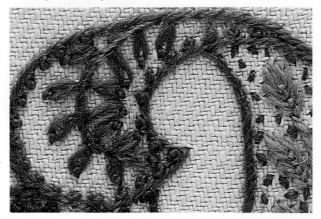

Bring the needle up through the fabric (1). Insert it in the same hole (2), forming a loop of thread as you do so, and bring the needle up in the loop (3), as shown. Pull the thread gently to make a rounded loop and catch it down with a small stitch (4). Detached chain stitches can be used on their own to fill an area or grouped to make flower shapes.

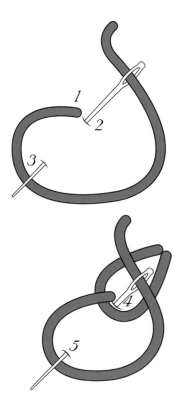

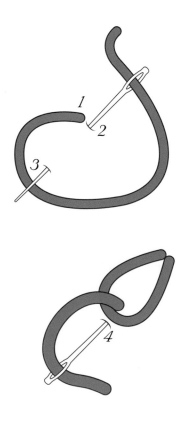

satin stitch

These are simply straight, flat stitches laid side by side. The length of the stitches will vary to fill the shape of the petal or leaf. Bring the needle up on one side of the shape (1). Insert it on the opposite side (2) and bring it back right next to the start of the first stitch (3). Always come up on the same side so that you cover the back of the fabric as well. This way your stitches will lie closely. To work a leaf with a central vein position the stitches closer together in the centre at the tip so that they radiate as they work around the end of the leaf.

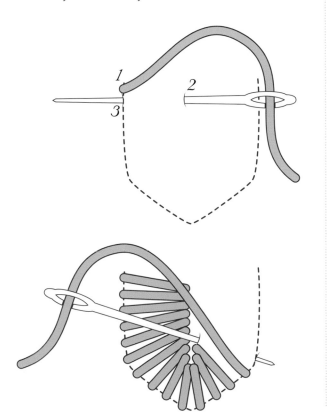

french knots

Bring your needle up through the fabric, hold the thread taut and wind the needle once around the thread (1). Pull the twist down on to the surface of the fabric and insert the needle into almost the same place as it came out but not quite or your knot will disappear through the hole (2). Pull the needle carefully through the fabric, keeping tension on the thread until you have to let go. (If you take the thread more than once around the needle you will tend to get a loose looking knot – if you want a larger knot use more strands of thread.)

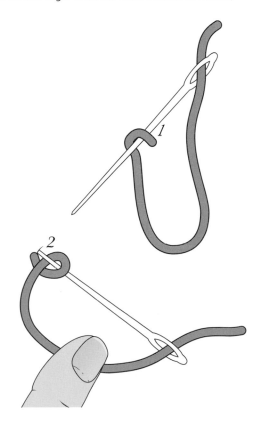

long-armed french knots

bullion knots

Bring your needle up through the fabric where you want the 'stalk' to begin (1). Wind the needle twice around the thread. Turn the needle point and insert it into the fabric where you want the knot to be (2). Pull the thread through to tighten the knot, holding it in place so that it doesn't unravel. You can make a circle of long-armed French knots by using the same hole to start each time.

The length of the finished coil of a bullion knot is determined by the length of the first stitch you make. Bring your needle up through the fabric at one end of the knot (1) and take it back down again where you want the knot to end (2). Bring the needle up through the first hole again but do not pull it through. Wind the loop around the needle several times until the length of the coil equals the length of the first stitch. Hold the thread coil and needle between your thumb and finger and gently but firmly pull the needle through. Allow the coil to turn back on itself and push the needle through the second hole to the back of your work.

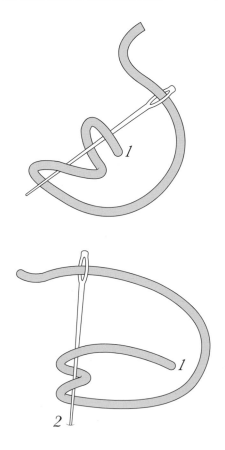

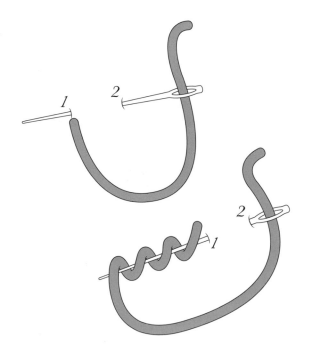

buttonhole stitch

Bring your needle up through the fabric on the line of the twisted edge (1). Push it back down through the fabric where the ends of the buttonhole stitch are to be (2) and then bring it up again just next to the first hole, passing it over the thread (3). Pull the thread gently so that the twisted edge sits neatly on the fabric, holding the tension on the thread with your other hand. Work the next stitch the required distance away, going down at 4 and up at 5. You can also work this stitch with long and short ends to lead into long and short stitch.

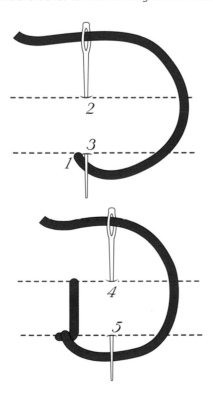

detached buttonhole stitch

Detached buttonhole stitch is worked into the looped edge of buttonhole stitch. It is worked in the same way as button-hole stitch but the stitches only pass into the loops of the buttonhole stitch, not into the fabric. It will help if you use a fine tapestry needle because the blunt end will pick up the loops more easily. This stitch adds a twisted frill to the original buttonhole twist.

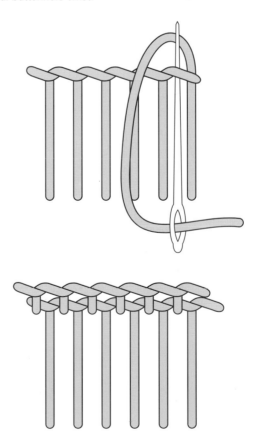

fly stitch

Make one long stitch at the tip of the shape. Bring your needle up just to the left of the top of this stitch (1). Go back down through the fabric just to the right of the first stitch (2) and bring the needle up through the same hole as the bottom of the first long stitch (3), catching the loop as you do so. Pull the loop gently so it sits neatly around the long stitch and catch it down with the smallest stitch you can make (4). Repeat until you have filled the shape. You may need to fill any odd bits left at the bottom with satin stitch if the vein reaches the bottom before the shape is filled. Work so closely that no fabric shows through your stitching.

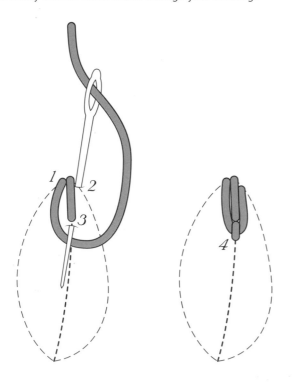

open fly stitch

Work this stitch in the same way as fly stitch but make the catching down stitch a long one. The width of the stitch can be varied to fill a shape but the fabric will show through. This stitch makes a lovely feathery line which is used to define the feathers on the parrot's tail, for example.

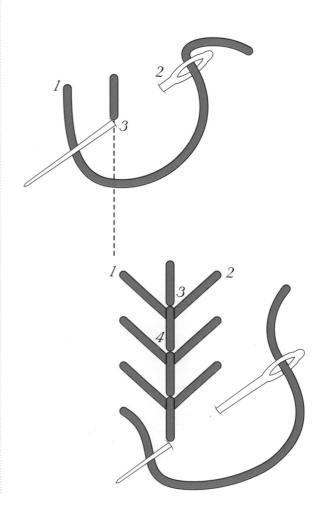

122

spider's web stitch

Start by working long stitches that cross at the centre of your circle with a crewel needle for the 'spokes'. Then bring your needle up very close to the centre. Change to a fine tapestry needle and work around the spokes as though you were working back stitch. Your needle should always pass under two spokes but not go into the fabric. Continue around the spokes until they are full, packing them well so that the whole thing rises up off the fabric.

straight spider's web stitch

Lay parallel bars across the area to be covered. Bring your needle up close to one end of the first bar. Change to a fine tapestry needle and make a loop round it. Repeat for each bar. Work up and down the bars, packing the weaving really tightly. As you pack the rows the stitch will start to rise up. If all the bars are not the same length leave them out as they become full and work shorter rows up and down.

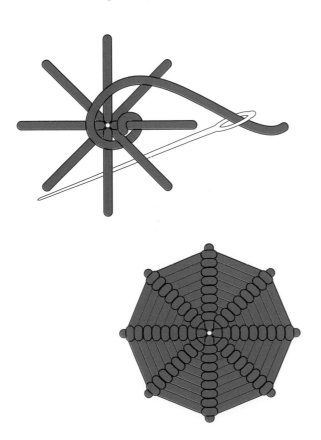

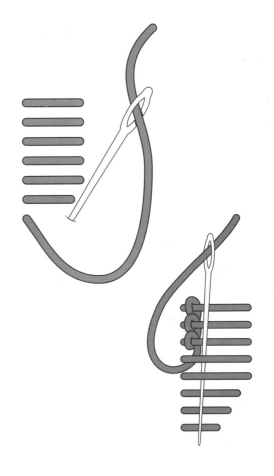

couching

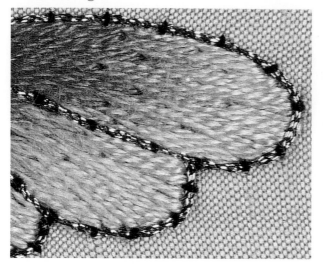

This is used for outlining and is usually the final touch on a design. Use two needles, one for the thread that you are laying and another for the tiny stitches that hold it down. Bring up the thread to be couched on the design line and lay it in place. Then work regularly spaced small stitches over it with the other thread, coming up at 1, going down at 2 and coming up again at 3. Take the couched thread to the back of the work when the whole section has been secured.

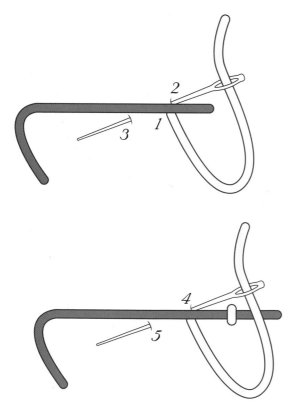

jacobean couching

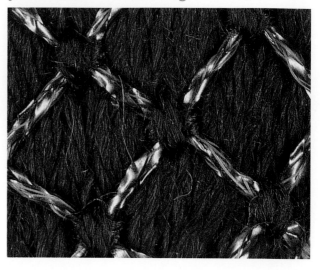

Lay a trellis of long stitches to fill the shape. Lay all the stitches in one direction first and then lay the ones in the other direction on top. You will find it easier if you lay the first thread in each direction across the middle of the shape and then fill to each side rather than trying to start with a short stitch across an edge. Couch down each intersection of the threads with a tiny upright cross stitch in a contrasting colour. This can be worked over an area first covered in long and short stitch to give a background colour or worked straight over the fabric for a more open effect.

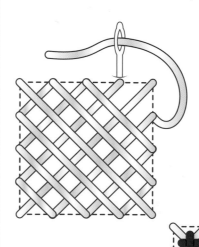

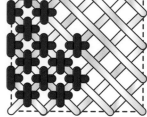

seeding

Seed stitches are tiny, evenly spaced back stitches, all at different angles to each other. When worked as back stitches rather than running stitches the resulting small stitches are rounded on the top of the fabric and will be more even. This is a very satisfying stitch to work but it takes a little practice to get a random effect. Come up at 1 and go down at 2, coming up at 3 ready to repeat the process.

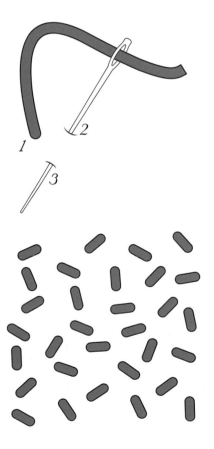

pearl stitch

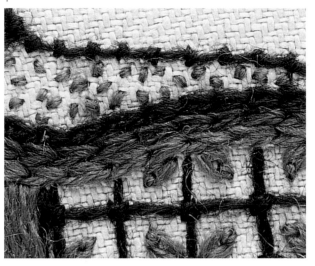

Bring your needle up on the design line (1) then take a small stitch a little way further along, bringing your needle up to the left at 3. Pass the needle under the stitch as shown. Repeat, working a small stitch which goes in at 4 and comes out at 5 and then pass the thread under the stitch as before. Continue working in this way.

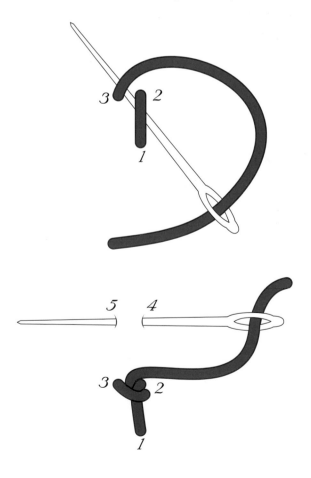

fern stitch

This is just a simple arrangement of straight stitches to make a fern-like frond with a delicate look. Always work the stitches from the ends of the fronds towards the main stem. Each of the fronds can also have branches. In this book the design outlines only provide the main 'stems' for the fern stitch. Work the little side ferns wherever you think they look right. To work the stitch come up at 1 and go down at 2, up at 3 and down at 1, etc.

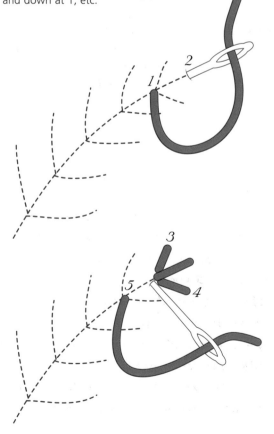

double cross stitch (star stitch)

This filling stitch can be randomly spaced or arranged in a pattern. Simply work a cross stitch and then work an upright cross stitch on top, placing your stitches exactly between the previous stitches. Take care that all the 'rays' are the same length or your stitching will not look neat. This stitch is particularly effective when combined with seeding.

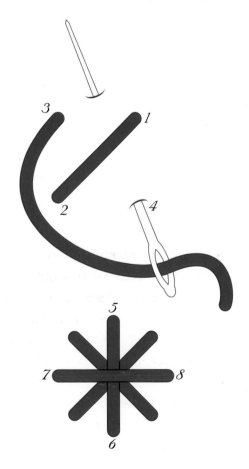

suppliers

Here is a list of suppliers and distributors which you should find helpful for tracking down the materials used in this book. Some of these companies are the manufacturers or distributors and should be able to give you the name and address of your local supplier.

Threads

DMC stranded cottons
DMC Creative World Ltd., Pullman Road, Wigston, Leicestershire LE18 2DY
Tel: 01533 811040

Appleton crewel wool
Appleton Bros, Thames Works, Church Street, Chiswick, London W4 2PE
Tel: 0181 994 0711

Caron Collection Soie Cristale
Macleod Craft Marketing, West Yonderton, Warlock Road, Bridge of Weir, Renfrewshire PA11 3SR
Tel: 01505 612618

Kreinik metallic braid
Coats Crafts UK, PO Box 22, The Lingfield Estate, McMullen Road, Darlington, Co Durham DL1 1YQ
Tel: 01325 365457

Cascade House Australian crewel wool
The Viking Loom Ltd., 22 High Petergate, York YO1 7EH
Tel: 01904 765599

21st Century Yarns Reflections hand-dyed silk
21st Century Yarns, Unit 9, Earl Soham Lodge, Earl Soham, Suffolk IP13 7SA
Tel: 01394 387659

Space-dyed threads
Stef Francis, Waverley, Higher Rocombe, Stokeinteinhead, Newton Abbot, Devon TQ12 4QL
Tel: 01803 323004

Fabrics

Linen twill
Ask in your local embroidery shop or I will sell it by mail order (see address below).

Silk dupion
Silken Threads, 36, Albion Street, Cheltenham, Gloucestershire GL52 2RQ
Tel: 01242 237773

Picture frames
Cleeve Picture Framing, Church Road, Bishops Cleeve, Cheltenham, Gloucestershire
Tel: 01242 672785

Other materials

Faux ivory bell pull ends and gold-plated embroidery needles
The Inglestone Collection, Yells Yard, Cirencester Road, Fairford, Gloucestershire GL7 4BS
Tel: 01285 712778

The lion and the unicorn workbox
Roland Bartlett, 25, Poplar Avenue, Markfield LE67 9WP
Tel: 01530 249288

Wooden pin-cushion base
Turnstyle, Alstons, Preston Wynne, Hereford HR1 3PA
Tel: 01432 820505

SUE HAWKINS has her own company, Needleworks, which produces counted canvaswork, crewelwork and cross stitch kits as well as upholstered embroidery frames. Ask your local shop for details or write (enclosing a stamped addressed envelope) to:

NEEDLEWORKS by Sue Hawkins, The Old School House, Hall Road, Leckhampton, Cheltenham, Gloucestershire GL53 0HP
Tel: 01242 584424

acknowledgments

My thanks are due to the following.

• My husband, John, who is always there for me with infinite patience, even when the broomstick comes out!

• Cheryl Brown at David and Charles for making it all possible. • Appleton for crewel wool in colours to die for.

• Jan Staniforth for stitching the bell pull so beautifully for me and instinctively knowing what I meant.

• Ethan Danielson for turning my scribbles into stitch diagrams.

• Tim and Zoe Hill and Jon and Barbara Stewart for their stunning photography.

• The ladies who attend my classes who didn't complain when I wouldn't let them come because I was working on this book.

• The Kit Company in Warminster who manufacture and distribute my embroidery kits so well and particularly to Chris Yard.

• Jane and Bill Greenoff – long may our friendship endure. • Cherry and Steve for lots of the fun in my life.

• Last, but not least, to my two spaniels who kept me company as I worked. Billy, who loves me unconditionally, hears all and divulges nothing and Tommy, his apprentice who has only just begun and sleeps on my feet as I finish.

index